PSYCHOLOGY OF SUCCESS
Developing Your Self-Esteem

The Career Education Division Student Success Series

Amos & Downes: The Successful Student's Guide to Career College
Amos & Downes: The Successful Student's Guide to Community College
Amos & Downes: The Successful Student's Guide to College
Beatrice: Learning to Study through Critical Thinking
Ferrett: Connections: Study Skills for College and Career Success
Ferrett: Peak Performance
Kitchens: Defeating Math Anxiety
Knight: Study Strategies for Careers
Knight: Study Strategies for College
Linville: ASAP: Academic Skills Achievement Program
Waitley: Psychology of Success: Developing Your Self-Esteem, Third Edition

P S Y C H O L O G Y
of
S U C C E S S

Developing Your Self-Esteem

Third Edition

DENIS WAITLEY, Ph.D.

GLENCOE
McGraw-Hill

New York, New York
Columbus, Ohio
Woodland Hills, California
Peoria, Illinois

Cover image: *Paysage en Provence,* Leo Gausson, © SuperStock

Copyright for the first edition was held by PAR, Incorporated.

Send all inquiries to:
Glencoe/McGraw-Hill
936 Eastwind Drive
Westerville, OH 43081

3 4 5 6 7 8 9   073/055   03 02 01 00 99

Library of Congress Cataloging-in-Publication Data

Waitley, Denis.
    Psychology of success : developing your self-esteem / Denis
Waitley. — 3rd ed.
      p.   cm.
    Includes bibliographical references (p. 257) and index.
    ISBN 0-256-19477-7
    1. Success—Psychological aspects.   2. Self-esteem.   3. Self
-confidence.   I. Title
BF637.S8W269   1997
    158'.1—dc20   96–3417

Preface

Psychology of Success is designed to teach students the fundamental psychological principles of success. In today's increasingly competitive job market, students need to begin their careers with confidence in themselves and their abilities. Unfortunately, many students lack this confidence, which is one of the most important qualities they will need to be successful in school and in the workplace. Students who enjoy confidence and self-esteem stay in school. They have the necessary tools to overcome obstacles in the way of their goals and dreams.

Who Can Use This Book

The third edition of *Psychology of Success* has been specifically oriented to students in career schools, vo-techs, and community colleges, but its principles are equally applicable to anyone who wants to increase his or her chances for success in life.

Benefits of the Book

Psychology of Success gets back to basics. Unlike many psychology books, this text does not expect students to change immediately the habits and thought processes of a lifetime. Students are asked to make changes for the better by first examining where they are now. In this respect, *Psychology of Success* is unique. It guides students along the path to success by examining important psychological qualities in a logical order. Students learn first how to assess who they are and how they feel about themselves. They develop a strong sense of self-awareness. Next, they learn about the importance of self-esteem and a positive self-image. Finally, through practical discussions, questions, and activities, students are taught how to set goals and work toward them. They are instructed in the importance of discipline and at the same time encouraged to dream.

Psychology of Success is a text that cheers students on even as it points out the necessity of hard work. The theme of the book can be summed up in the word *win*. Students are encouraged to make the effort for themselves. Again and again, they are assured that their victory lies in the attempt, not the final outcome. With this supportive tone, *Psychology of Success* makes it easier for students to take risks, without the fear of failure.

Skills Students Will Develop

As they read and work through the text, students will learn how to develop the psychological qualities necessary for success, as well as the following skills, including how to:

- Assess their strengths and weaknesses.
- Choose healthy responses to stress and anger.
- Manage their time.
- Take responsibility for their actions.
- Set goals and develop a plan for achieving them.
- Motivate themselves.
- Make a positive first impression.
- Communicate effectively.
- Treat themselves and others with respect.

Pedagogical Features

The features of this book have been developed to give the material an immediate relevance for students. The following descriptions help explain how they work:

Opening Quote: The opening quote sums up the ideas that will be discussed in the chapter, in a way that stimulates students' curiosity and is in itself food for thought.

Chapter Objectives: The chapter objectives give a focus to the chapter from the start and let students know the kinds of skills and information they can expect to have mastered after having read the text and completed the activities.

Vignette (Scene 1): The student vignettes have been written to illustrate the problems and challenges being faced by fictitious students who, as yet, have not mastered the psychological principle of that particular chapter. First we are introduced to the student and learn about his or her situation. Then we hear the student's own narrative—the thoughts, fears, and feelings he or she has while searching for a solution to the problem at hand. The feelings they express in the vignettes will cause the students reading the text to identify strongly with the characters and provoke a "This could be me" response.

A Talk with Dr. Waitley: In this section, students get a lesson in the principles of success from one of the world's foremost authorities on personal achievement. Dr. Waitley explains his concept of winning and introduces students to the basic psychological qualities that are necessary for success. He gives students a thorough grounding in the key issues that lead to self-confidence.

Winning with . . . : Here, the principles examined by Dr. Waitley are discussed in a wider context. Students read about the viewpoints of other experts and learn how the popular view of these principles has changed through the years. Dr. Waitley's teachings are further explained and expanded upon, and students are given many practical suggestions for incorporating these principles into their daily lives.

Thought-Provoking Questions: These five questions challenge students to think about the information they've just learned in new ways. These questions are equally effective when read by an individual or used for a classroom discussion. One question in each set, identified with an ink pen icon, provides the basis for a journal writing exercise, encouraging introspection while providing students with an opportunity to exercise and enhance their writing skills.

Vignette (Scene 2): In the last half of the vignette, the student in the story has begun to grasp the psychological principle that he or she had been lacking, and finds a solution to his or her problem, taking the kind of positive steps exemplified in the book. The vignettes stress a balance between solving problems on one's own and seeking help from others.

Strategies for Success: These write-in activities provide concrete steps for students to begin using their new-found knowledge. Some activities call for specific responses while others encourage the student to create his or her own answers. Many of the activities provide additional suggestions for ways students can continue to apply their new insights to their daily lives.

≈ *Acknowledgments*

This book would not have been possible without the help and support of many people. The following reviewers offered invaluable and greatly appreciated advice on the development of this manuscript:

Cynthia A. Hilden	Blue Mountain Community College
Donna N. Knapp	New Kensington Commercial School
Michael R. Mobly	DeMarge College
Ruth A. Ott	Stautzenberger College
Laurie S. Restivo	Alaska Computer Institute
Judith A. Smith	Anson Community College
David C. Wells	Muskingum Area Technical College
Tracy Willems	Stratton College

Additional thanks go to Penworthy—especially to Gayle Entrup—for contributions to the development of this third edition.

And finally, my thanks to the entire Career Education Division for their support, assistance, and encouragement.

Denis Waitley

To the Student

This book may well be one of the most important ones you ever read. Certainly it can help you make some important changes in your life, changes that can lead you down the road to success.

You are being taught many valuable skills that will help you find and keep the job you want. The skills talked about in this book are unique because they can't be taught. You have to learn them for yourself. They are the skills that help you develop confidence in yourself and your abilities. Self-confidence is one of the most important elements of success. It helps determine how successful you will be at school, at work, and at life.

In this book you'll learn specific skills that will help you develop the personal qualities you need for success. You'll take a good look at yourself and where you are right now. You'll learn about discipline and work, as well as goals and dreams and having fun. Most important, you'll discover the Winner inside you.

As you work through this book, you'll read about people who made changes in their lives. They set new goals and achieved them. A lot of these people were students just like you. They learned that winning means making the most of themselves, and being the best they can be. Now it's your turn to win—and be the best you can be.

About the Author

Denis Waitley is a world-renowned expert and motivational speaker on human performance and potential. Best known as the author/ narrator of *The Psychology of Winning*, he has helped millions of people throughout the world in their quest for personal excellence. He is the author of several best-selling books, including *Seeds of Greatness, The Winner's Edge, Being the Best,* and *Empires of the Mind.*

Long recognized as an authority on high-level achievement, Dr. Waitley has counseled leaders in every field, from CEOs to Super-bowl champions. He has lent his understanding and expertise to both American astronauts and POWs. During the 1980s Dr. Waitley was a member of the U.S. Olympic Committee's Sports Medicine Council, dedicated to the performance enhancement of Olympic athletes.

One of the country's most sought-after speakers, Denis Waitley was recently named Outstanding Platform Speaker of the year by his peers and elected to the International Speakers' Hall of Fame. A grad-uate of the U.S. Naval Academy at Annapolis, he holds a doctorate in human behavior. Currently a board member of the National Council on Self-Esteem, he is also a consultant to the President's Council on Vocational Education and the International Parenting Association.

Contents

CHAPTER 1   *Psychology of Success: An Introduction*   3

Self-WHAT?   4
What Do Those Words Mean?   4
Chapter Preview   4
Using This Book   5
    Opening Quote   5
    Chapter Objectives   5
    Scene 1   6
    A Talk with Dr. Waitley   6
    Winning with . . .   6
    Marginal Notes   6
    Key Words   6
    Scene 2   6
    Thought-Provoking Questions   7
    Strategies for Success   7
Anything Else?   7
What Are We Waiting for?   7

CHAPTER 2   *Psychology of Self-Awareness*   9

Chapter Objectives   9
Scene 2–1: *Karen's Story,* "*Do I really belong here?*"   10
A Talk with Dr. Waitley   12
What Is Self-Awareness?   12
Environmental Self-Awareness   12
    Empathy   13
    Adapting   14

Physical Self-Awareness   14

   Stress   14

   Anger   15

Mental Self-Awareness   16

Winning with Self-Awareness   17

The Importance of Self-Awareness   17

Developing Environmental Self-Awareness   17

   Feeling Empathy   18

   Adapting to Change   18

Improving Physical Self-Awareness   19

   Dealing with Stress   19

   Dealing with Anger   22

Creating Mental Self-Awareness   23

Scene 2–2: *Karen's Story, Karen is more self-aware and self-confident.*   26

Thought-Provoking Questions   28

Activity 2–1: Increasing Self-Awareness   29

Activity 2–2: Balanced Living   33

Activity 2–3: Wheel of Life   35

Activity 2–4: Stress Test   37

Activity 2–5: Personal Stressors and Relievers   41

CHAPTER 3   *Psychology of Self-Image*   45

Chapter Objectives   45

Scene 3–1: *Paul's Story, "What if I'm not smart enough?"*   46

A Talk with Dr. Waitley   48

What Is Self-Image?   48

The History of Your Self-Image   48

   Blue-Eyed, Brown Eyed   48

   Self-Defeating Attitudes   49

   Labels   49

Imagination   50

Your Subconscious Min   51

A Winning Self-Image   51

Winning with a Positive Self-Image   53

The Importance of a Positive Self-Image   53

Creating Your Self-Image   53

   Searching for Identity   54

   Ideals   54

Developing Your Creativity   55

   Self-Image and Creativity   56

   Visualization   56

Scene 3–2: *Paul's Story,   Paul chooses a new self-image.*   58

Thought-Provoking Questions   60

Activity 3–1: Imagine That . . .   61

Activity 3–2: The Pen Pal   63

Activity 3–3: Admire a Hero   65

Activity 3–4: Dream Job   67

Activity 3–5: Admire Me   71

CHAPTER 4   *Psychology of Self-Esteem*   73

Chapter Objectives   73

Scene 4–1: *Sarah's Story,   "Have I made the right decision?"*   74

A Talk with Dr. Waitley   76

What Is Self-Esteem?   76

Learning to Like Yourself   76

A Lifetime Program   77

Self-Worth   77

Focusing on Success   77

Self-Talk   78

Winning with Self-Esteem   80

The Importance of Self-Esteem   80

Studying Self-Esteem   80

   Low Self-Esteem   80

   High Self-Esteem   81

Feeling Good about Others, Too   81

Building Your Self-Esteem   82

   Recognizing and Overcoming Barriers to Positive Self-Esteem   82

   Developing Strategies to Improve Self-Esteem   84

   Remembering Past Success and Forgetting Past Failure   84

   Creating a Personal Support System   85

Signs of Self-Worth   85

Scene 4–2: *Sarah's Story,   Sarah builds up her self-esteem.*   86

Thought-Provoking Questions   88

Activity 4–1: Test Your Self-Esteem   89

Activity 4–2: Your Values   95

Activity 4–3: Do You Resist Change?   97

Activity 4–4: Positive Self-Talk   101

Activity 4–5: U-Turns Allowed   103

CHAPTER 5   *Psychology of Self-Discipline*   107

Chapter Objectives   107

Scene 5–1: *Rick's Story,   "Where do I begin?"*   108

A Talk with Dr. Waitley   110

What Is Self-Discipline?   110

The Desire to Change   110

See the Experience   110

Against the Odds   111

Self-Talk   111

You Make It Happen   112

Play Your Hand   112

Winning with Self-Discipline   114

The Importance of Self-Discipline   114

Making Choices   114

Breaking Bad Habits   116

Taking Responsibility   117

Getting Support   118

Choosing Positive Attitudes   118

Scene 5–2: *Rick's Story,   Rick learns to organize his time.*   120

Thought-Provoking Questions   122

Activity 5–1: Time-Demand Survey   123

Activity 5–2: Using Self-Discipline   127

Activity 5–3: Overcoming Obstacles   131

Activity 5–4: Attendance Chart   135

Activity 5–5: To-Do Chart   137

CHAPTER 6   *Psychology of Self-Motivation*   141

Chapter Objectives   141

Scene 6–1: *Diane's Story,   "What difference does it make?"*   142

A Talk with Dr. Waitley   144

What Is Self-Motivation?   144

Positive Tension   145

Risk as Opportunity   145

The Winner's Edge   146

Modern-Day Heroes   147
Winning with Self-Motivation   148
The Importance of Self-Motivation   148
Some Views on Motivation   148
Values and Motivation   149
Examining Your Goals   150
Self-Talk   151
Visualization   151
The Comfort Zone   152
The Fear Of Failure   153
Procrastination   153
Working toward Success   154
Motivation from Others   155
Scene 6–2: *Diane's Story,   Diane finds the motivation she needs.* 156
Thought-Provoking Questions   158
Activity 6–1: Positive Self-Talk   159
Activity 6–2: Standing Your Ground   163
Activity 6–3: Personal Motivation   167
Activity 6–4: Success at Work   169
Activity 6–5: Positive Projection   175

CHAPTER 7   *Psychology of Self-Direction*   179

Chapter Objectives   179
Scene 7–1: *Jason's Story,   "Where do I go from here?"*   180
A Talk with Dr. Waitley   182
What Is Self-Direction?   182
Who Are the Winners?   183
A Purpose in Life   183
What Are Goals?   184
Lifetime Goals   185
Happiness   185
Winning with Self-Direction   186
The Importance of Self-Direction   186
Short-Term and Long-Term Goals   186
Dealing with Problems   187
Time Management   188
Handling Big Projects   189
Punctuality   190

Money Management   190

Self-Direction and Happiness   191

　Personal Happiness   191

　A Look on the Bright Side   192

Scene 7–2: *Jason's Story,   Jason moves in the right direction.*   194

Thought-Provoking Questions   196

Activity 7–1: Procrastination   197

Activity 7–2: Draw a Tree   199

Activity 7–3: SMART Goals   201

Activity 7–4: Look Who's Making Headlines   205

Activity 7–5: It's About Time!   207

CHAPTER 8   *Psychology of Self-Projection*   213

Chapter Objectives   213

Scene 8–1: *Sheila's Story,   "What's the use?"*   214

A Talk With Dr. Waitley   216

What Is Self-Projection?   216

Prepare for Success   216

Stress and Success   217

The Drug of Optimism   217

Projecting Self-Worth   218

　Your Appearance   218

　Verbal Communication   219

　Nonverbal Communication   219

　A Winning First Impression   220

The Values of a Winner   220

Winning with Self-Projection   221

The Importance of Self-Projection   221

Projecting Good Health   221

Projecting Success   222

Making a Good Impression   222

　Appearance   223

　Verbal Communication   223

　Nonverbal Communication   224

Make Your Own Luck   224

What Would a Winner Do?   225

Get Ready for Success   225

Scene 8–2: *Sheila's Story,   Sheila projects confidence and finds success.*   228

Thought-Provoking Questions   230

Activity 8–1: Communication   231

Activity 8–2: Communication and Relationships   233

Activity 8–3: Self-Improvement   235

Activity 8–4: Dealing with Problems   237

Activity 8–5: The Wheel of Life Comes Full Circle, Part 1   239

CHAPTER 9   *Psychology of Success: Looking Back, Looking Ahead*   243

What Is Success?   244

The Principles of a Winner   244

Join the Winners' Circle!   247

Thought-Provoking Questions   249

Activity 9–1: The Wheel of Life Comes Full Circle, Part 2   251

Scene 9–1:   *Jack's Story,   Portrait of a Winner*   254

Select Bibliography   257

Glossary   259

Index   261

PSYCHOLOGY OF SUCCESS
Developing Your Self-Esteem

What lies behind us and what lies before us are small matters compared to what lies within us.

Ralph Waldo Emerson

C H A P T E R

1

Psychology of Success: An Introduction

You are about to begin the most interesting and perhaps the most rewarding study of your life. You are going to study about YOU! You will look at your hopes, dreams, goals, and the ways that you can achieve every one of them.

Self-WHAT?

You will notice that this book is entirely about you. Your self. You may not be familiar with some of the concepts now, but after you finish reading this book and completing the activities, you will know more about the following principles:

- Self-awareness
- Self-image
- Self-esteem
- Self-discipline
- Self-motivation
- Self-direction
- Self-projection

You will also have applied each of those concepts to your own life.

What Do Those Words Mean?

Don't let the terms intimidate you. They are just words that mean looking at yourself, finding all the good within you, and developing all the potential that you have to be the best you can be. In other words, you will become a Winner!

You will learn that you can set your own limits and shouldn't let others set limitations for you. What does that mean? It means that you can go just as far as you want to go; you don't have to stop where someone else says you will.

Chapter Preview

For every goal we have in life, we will learn there are a series of steps we must follow to achieve it. It is the same with our goal of personal success. This book is divided into seven chapters of steps that you will need to follow in achieving personal success.

Chapter 2, Psychology of Self-Awareness, will help you to become more aware of yourself and how you relate to circumstances and people around you.

Chapter 3, Psychology of Self-Image, will help you to see your true self, not just the one that you and everyone around you has come to accept.

Chapter 4, Psychology of Self-Esteem, will help you to have confidence in yourself and be satisfied with yourself.

Chapter 5, Psychology of Self-Discipline, will help you to do the things that are necessary to reach your goals without becoming side-tracked by bad habits.

Chapter 6, Psychology of Self-Motivation, will help you to find the desire to move into action to achieve your goals.

Chapter 7, Psychology of Self-Direction, will help you to set a well-defined goal and work toward it.

Chapter 8, Psychology of Self-Projection, will help you to use your confidence and optimism to make good things happen.

Using This Book

Each chapter has the same features to help you learn more about the specific topic. Let's explore those features.

Opening Quote

Before you begin reading each chapter, read the opening quote and give some thought to what you think it means. Give yourself a few uninterrupted minutes to relax and open your mind to the topic in that chapter.

Chapter Objectives

These objectives or goals will give you a focus to your study of the chapter. They let you know what each chapter expects to be able to do for you and what you will be able to do after completing the reading and the activities. You may be able to complete some of the objectives right away but may need more time to accomplish others.

Scene 1

Each chapter introduces you to someone who may or may not be like you and may or may not be facing the same type of problems you are. This person, in all chapters, needs some help dealing with a problem related to personal success. As you read these stories, keep an open mind and think how you might solve the problem if you were that person.

A Talk with Dr. Waitley

These pages allow you to have a one-on-one session with one of the leading authorities on personal success. Pretend that you are alone with Dr. Waitley as he gives you information and guidance in becoming a Winner. Dr. Waitley has faith in you and so does your instructor. Dr. Waitley has helped many people find the Winners that were hiding inside. Let him help you find yours!

Winning with . . .

This part of the chapter will take the principles that Dr. Waitley has introduced to you and give you more information on how to apply them to your life. Here is where you will learn how to become a Winner.

Marginal Notes

Marginal notes will be included in both the talk with Dr. Waitley and the rest of the chapter. You may use the marginal notes to preview the material before you begin and to review the material after you finish. They can be reminders to you of how you can achieve your personal success.

Key Words

When key words are used for the first time, they are printed in bold type and defined for you. These are terms that you should become familiar with and apply to your own life.

Scene 2

Remember the person that you met at the beginning of the chapter? We take another look and show how the principles from the chapter can be applied to that person's situation. By seeing how that person deals with obstacles, you may see how you can, too.

Thought-Provoking Questions

These questions are meant to challenge you to think a little bit more about the topics in the chapter. They are not review questions where there is definitely a right or wrong answer. Be creative and open to the ideas that these questions may introduce to you.

Included in the questions for every chapter is one question that is appropriate for you to write about in a personal journal. A pen icon identifies each of these questions. Have you ever kept a journal or diary before? It doesn't have to be something fancy with a lock and key. However, it should be some type of notebook that you can use only as your journal and be something that can be kept private. This is your chance to talk to yourself and record your thoughts, hopes, and dreams. At the end of the term, you will be able to look back through your journal and see how much you have grown. You will have proof of your development into a Winner!

Strategies for Success

At the end of each chapter are several activities that you should complete to help you better understand the ideas you have read about. These activities will help you to apply the principles to your life and really make this book just for you.

Anything Else?

This book also features a bibliography following Chapter 9. You may want to use this list of books as a starting point to do more reading about achieving personal success. You should be able to buy the books in any bookstore; many of them may be available to you at your school or local public library. As you examine some of these titles on the shelf, also look at other books in the same area. You can learn as much about winning as you allow yourself to.

Have trouble remembering the definition of a term? Can't remember which chapter it was in? Look in the glossary provided at the back of the book. All the key terms from each chapter have been included for your reference.

What Are We Waiting For?

Let's get started! Chapter 2 will help you to explore your unique potential and set you on your journey to become a Winner.

The great thing in this world is not so much where we stand as in what direction we are moving.

Oliver Wendell Holmes, Sr

2

Psychology of Self-Awareness

After you read this chapter and complete the activities, you will:

- Be more aware of yourself and those around you.

- Be more aware of your environment and feel empathy with others you meet.

- Be more physically self-aware and able to handle stress and anger in healthy ways.

- Be more aware of your own potential and the need for self-honesty.

S C E N E

2–1

☞

K A R E N ' S   S T O R Y

"Do I really belong here?"

Karen walked into the classroom, finally, having gone down the wrong hallway. She was hungry and had a headache. She had really been looking forward to this day, but now she was wondering if she had made a mistake.

Everyone else seemed so sure of themselves. Karen began to feel herself getting angry with the school for hiding the classroom, the other students for finding the room and getting to class before her, and even the instructor for not greeting the students at the door.

Karen was 31 years old and had been working for the past seven years as a receptionist and general office worker for a small accounting firm. Although she liked her job, she didn't see any chance for advancement. She began to wonder where her life was going. She didn't want to be stuck the rest of her life in a dead-end job. She wanted more out of life.

It seemed to her that the people she'd gone to high school with were all more successful than she was. The accountants in the firm all seemed to be getting younger; when they reached her age, they were moving on to bigger firms and better jobs with higher salaries. So Karen decided to go back to school to earn a degree in accounting. This was her first accounting class.

As Karen took the last seat in the classroom, she began to question her decision to come back to school. Did she belong here? After all, she did like her job . . .

Had Karen made a mistake, or was she just feeling the stress of the first day?

Dr. Waitley discusses the principle of self-awareness, as well as awareness of your environment and awareness of other people.

What Is Self-Awareness?

Every individual is unique, with the potential to be a Winner.

One of the most important elements of success is self-awareness. **Self-awareness** is the ability to step back from the canvas of life and take a good look at yourself as you relate to your environmental, physical, and mental worlds. It is the ability to accept yourself as a unique, changing, imperfect, and growing individual. It is the ability to recognize your potential as well as your limitations.

Self-awareness is also self-honesty, which is the ability to see all your strengths and weaknesses clearly. It is knowing what you have to offer and recognizing that time and effort will be necessary for top achievement. Winners can look in the mirror and see what lies behind their own eyes. You are a Winner when what you think, how you feel, and what you do all fit together.

Environmental Self-Awareness

Winners are aware and accepting of the world around them.

Winners display an environmental self-awareness. They are aware of how little they really know about anything in their world. They realize that their heredity and environment affect what they know and how they think. Winners are able to accept what is happening around them, and this ability contributes to their self-awareness. This awareness includes being concerned about the needs of others.

Are you open-minded? Do you look at life through your parents' eyes? Did you develop your own prejudices or did you inherit them from your parents? **Environmental self-awareness** means realizing that each human being on earth is a person with the equal right to fulfill his or her own potential in life. It is realizing that skin color, religion, birthplace, financial status, or intelligence do not determine a person's worth or value. Environmental self-awareness is accepting the fact that every human being is a unique individual. No two people are exactly alike—even identical twins.

Have you ever heard someone say, "We're not on the same wavelength"? This translates to: "You don't think as I do," or "I don't understand why you think the way you do." It is easy to see why there is so much misunderstanding and fighting in the world, within families, and among nations. Everyone sees life through a different camera lens and "marches to the beat of a different drummer."

Empathy

Empathy is the awareness of and sensitivity to the feelings, thoughts, and experiences of others. It is seeing life through other persons' eyes—experiencing their pain, curiosity, hopes, and fears. It is watching marathon runners at the 20-mile mark and feeling your own legs ache.

You can feel empathy with anyone—whether that person is of a different generation, a citizen of another country, or simply someone with a different point of view. Instead of being quick to criticize or judge other persons, try to see the situation through their eyes. How do they feel? What are they afraid of? What concerns them most?

Perform this "Empathy Checkup" on yourself by changing places with someone else:

Winners can look at any situation from both their own and others' points-of-view.

- *If I were my husband or wife, how would I feel about having a partner like me?* Would I think I was supportive? Independent? Interesting? Understanding? An equal partner?

- *If I were my child, how would I feel about having a parent like me?* Would I think I was patient? Encouraging? Positive? Supportive? Nonjudgmental?

- *If I were my instructor, how would I feel about having a student like me?* Would I think I showed a lot of effort? A lot of interest? Curiosity? Discipline? Concern for others in class?

- *If I were my boss, how would I feel about having an employee like me?* Would I think I was a good worker? Productive? Reliable? Responsible? Nice to work with?

- *How would it feel to be an immigrant who has just arrived in America?* Would I feel isolated? Frightened? Unsure of whom to trust? Challenged? Optimistic? Hopeful?

- *How does the world appear through the eyes of a child?* Big? Confusing? Exciting? Scary? Hard to understand? Fun?

Adapting

*Winners keep an open
mind in new situations.*

Does it bother you to discover that there are so many people around
who are different from you? Do you think you might seem strange or
different to other people? We need to understand what being human
is all about. To be human is to be a changing, growing, imperfect, but
amazing living creation. Winners know they will come across many
different people, places, and experiences in their lifetimes. A lot of
those people, places, and experiences will seem very strange and
unfamiliar. How can you learn to enjoy all the different and unusual
things that you come across in life?

The answer is to adapt. **Adapting** means being flexible and
open to the actions of others. Because Winners are self-aware and
have empathy for others, they do not allow others to ruin their day
or rain on their parade. Adapting to our environment means being
flexible and changing with the times as we need to.

Physical Self-Awareness

*Winners do their best to
take good care of their
bodies.*

Our next step is to develop our physical self-awareness. **Physical
self-awareness** means understanding that our bodies are machines
whose performance depends on good health. We must each treat our
body as our one and only transportation vehicle for life. We must
care for it with the fuel of good nutrition, activity, and health care.
If we are fat and sluggish or thin and nervous because we smoke,
drink, eat poorly, or don't exercise, we cannot trade in our bodies for
new models. If we abuse them, we won't be able to use them as long
or as well. You can do well only if you feel well.

Stress

Stress is any physical, emotional, or chemical factor that causes tension. Stress can have both positive and negative results. Earl Nightingale, a well-known motivational speaker, told the story of a trip he
took with his son to the Great Barrier Reef, which stretches 1,800
miles from New Guinea to Australia. He noticed that the coral growing on the inside of the reef, where the sea was peaceful and quiet in
the lagoon, looked pale and lifeless. The coral on the outside of the
reef, however, constantly beaten by the powerful waves, looked
healthy and brightly colored. Earl asked the guide why this was so.
"It is very simple," came the reply. "The coral on the lagoon side dies
rapidly with no challenge for growth and survival, while the coral
facing the open sea thrives and multiplies because it is challenged
and tested every day."

Winners use stress as a challenge to succeed.

So it is with all living things on earth. If we never challenge ourselves, we never have the opportunity to succeed. We can choose to just sit back and wither on the vine, or we can use the failures and setbacks in our lives to strengthen ourselves and help us guard against anxiety, depression, and other negative responses to stress.

Not much has changed since the days of our early ancestors when, at the first sign of danger, the body became ready for "fight or flight." A person would either fight against danger or run the other way. Nowadays, we experience at least one or two unpleasant surprises almost every day, and we have to make the decision to fight or walk the other way.

Dr. Hans Selye, one of the first people to study stress, divides people into two categories: racehorses and turtles. A racehorse loves to run and will die from exhaustion if it is corralled or confined in a small space. A turtle will die from exhaustion if forced to run on a treadmill, moving too fast for its slow nature. We each have to find our own healthy stress level, somewhere between that of the racehorse and the turtle.

Anger

How many complete strangers got you upset and ready to risk your life on the road today? Winners don't overreact as the cave dwellers did to what is happening. Winners are not quick to anger, with their blood pressures jumping, heart rates quickening, and adrenaline pumping. Every annoying situation is not a struggle for survival, and there are not always tigers ready to pounce.

Winners find strategies to help them deal with anger.

Winners don't let daily stress destroy their mental and physical health. They don't drink more, smoke more, or pop more pills to escape or cope with the stress. They don't take their anger out on other people. They control their negative feelings and express them in a constructive way. When Winners feel angry or upset, they do anything that will relieve their negative feelings in a healthy way, such as jogging around the block, taking a long walk, or listening to some soothing music. Self-awareness is an important part of the victory over stress. Winners learn how to relax and cope with the ups and downs of everyday life.

Expressing joy, love, compassion, and excitement is healthy. However, openly expressing hostility, anger, depression, loneliness, or anxiety may not be healthy. The only healthy expression of the "fight or flight" response is in the face of a life or death situation. In most daily situations, stress and anger can be dealt with by deep breathing, relaxation, and exercise such as running, aerobics, or basketball.

Mental Self-Awareness

Winners challenge the potential within their minds.

An important part of positive self-awareness is mental self-aware-ness. **Mental self-awareness** is knowing the potential within our own minds that is just waiting to be challenged. We must ask ourselves, "What is my mental outlook toward life? Do I sell myself short, or am I overconfident in my abilities?"

Truth and honesty are necessary for any real and lasting success. We must ask ourselves: "Is this true? Is this honest?" If we can answer yes, or if we can seek out the truth with the help of someone else, we can move ahead and take action.

Attitude is the key to healthy self-awareness. In order to feel well and accomplish things in your life, you'll need to develop posi-tive attitudes and positive responses to the pressures in life. The more honest and self-aware you become, the more ways you'll find to win. Find a new way to win today!

Let's take a closer look at some of the points Dr. Waitley discussed and learn how to use the principle of self-awareness in our everyday lives.

The Importance of Self-Awareness

Develop self-awareness by observing how you function in the world around you.

Self-awareness is being conscious of yourself in the world around you. It is understanding yourself as you function in your environments. Health and well-being depend on being conscious of what is happening to you physically and mentally in ways that you may or may not be able to control.

Current thinking backs up Dr. Waitley's teachings about self-awareness and its importance in our lives. Other psychologists and writers have explored the subject and given us additional ideas on this principle.

Libraries and bookstores are excellent sources of self-awareness materials. Magazine articles provide many questions to create self-awareness on a variety of topics. Readers seem eager to learn more about their "personality types." This interest is simply a need for improved self-awareness.

Developing Environmental Self-Awareness

It is interesting that being aware of yourself often means first becoming aware of what is around you.

Your environments include home, school, work, and community.

Environmental self-awareness concerns your relationships with the world—your family, friends, and community—as well as your responsibility as a citizen of the planet Earth. When you see yourself as part of a larger whole, you have respect for what is around you. A Winner has self-respect and respect for the environment. Winners understand the importance of clean air, clean water, and all the resources that we depend on. When you value and respect your surroundings, you can start working to improve them. When you improve your surroundings, you improve your quality of life as well.

Thinkers have explored the idea of the "self" in an effort to better understand how we work within our environments. The philosopher Alan Watts, who wrote in the late 1950s and 1960s about ideas from India, China, and Japan, believed that we should not think of ourselves as separate beings trying to control the outside world. Instead, he said, let's think of ourselves as part of that world.

Respecting the environment can include recycling so that products may be reused. Buying things made from recycled materials is helpful. By limiting our use of certain chemicals, we can improve the quality of the air we breathe. What can you do to improve your environment today?

Understanding yourself and being conscious of the world around you contribute to your overall sense of well-being.

Feeling Empathy

Empathy means being aware of and sensitive to what the other person is feeling.

Self-awareness can help you look beyond yourself for meaning and honesty. When you see yourself as part of a larger picture, you become concerned about the others in that picture. Being aware means knowing when others need help. It is reaching out a hand to lift them up. It is an idea that Dr. Waitley calls the double win—If I help you win, then I win too.

Dr. Waitley talked about empathy and feeling emotions that others feel—having the ability to see through others' eyes. By feeling these emotions, we are each able to control our attitudes, responses, and actions so that we don't hurt other people's feelings.

You may have now (and will have in the future) many roles in your life: student, employee, parent, relative, friend. In each of these roles it helps to feel empathy for others. For instance, suppose another student in your class isn't learning the course material as well as you are. What is your response? Someone without empathy might say, "Pat's just not with it and doesn't understand anything. What a loser." However, when you empathize with someone, you can say, "Poor Pat. I know what it is like to feel a little confused sometimes in class. I hope Pat will ask our instructor for extra help." If you were the student having problems, how would you want others to respond?

Adapting to Change

Change adds variety to life.

Being flexible and open to the actions of others can make life an exciting and enjoyable experience. People who choose not to adapt to new ideas can become bored with life or disappointed with everyday occurrences. What if you would only eat a peanut butter sandwich every day for lunch? You might never enjoy a hamburger, taco, pizza, or gyro. No lunch is more "right"; each lunch is "different" and can be enjoyed for those differences. The same can be true for any change in your family, home, school, or job. You can choose to make the best of any situation and enjoy your new experiences.

Improving Physical Self-Awareness

Make healthy choices: good food, exercise, and adequate rest.

As Dr. Waitley discussed, self-awareness includes physical self-awareness. Physical self-awareness is being aware of your body's needs—giving it all the good food, exercise, and rest it requires. It means making healthy choices for your body because you want to be fit for life. When you take care of yourself physically, it is easier for you to deal with many other stresses in life. A healthy body is less likely to catch colds or tire easily.

Studies have shown that we can control our bodies' reactions to many stressful situations. If our minds can control how our bodies react to stress, then it follows that, by relaxing our bodies, we can relax our minds.

Dealing with Stress

Dr. Waitley mentioned Dr. Hans Selye, who did some studies on the effects of stress. Selye studied people's stress levels and compared them to "racehorses" and "turtles." He conducted more studies, this time with lab animals. He noted their reactions to intense heat, loud noises, bright lights, and other stressful experiences. He noted that the animals had physical reactions to high levels of stress. Some even developed ulcers.

This kind of study makes us more aware of the ways in which stress can affect our own bodies. The animals in the experiment were subjected to "bad" stress. People recognize both "good" and "bad" types of stress. Good, or positive, stress pumps us up. It feels good. It is fun to get excited watching a football game. It is nice to look forward to a big party. Winners know that positive stress can be good for them. Unpleasant or upsetting events cause "bad" stress. A lot of negative stresses can be unhealthy.

Have you ever noticed how different people can react to the same event in different ways? You may feel excited about trying to do your best on an exam while your friend might feel nervous and tense. Another friend might not feel one way or the other.

Your body's responses to stress overload can be physical or emotional. You may have frequent headaches, experience heart palpitations, tight muscles, ringing in your ears, or sweaty palms. You may find yourself crying easily or feeling nervous, overwhelmed, powerless, or angry.

In stressful or anger-causing situations, you have a lot more control than you might think. You can choose your emotions. It is not so much what happens to you that matters as how you react to what happens. If you see a situation as hopeless, you may experience depression. If you see every situation as hopeless, you might react with an "escape response."

An **escape response** is an action or behavior that helps get your mind off your troubles. A positive escape response might be to go for a walk or talk with a friend. A positive response makes you feel better for a while, in a constructive way. You act in a way that does not harm you or add to the problem.

Negative escape responses include overeating, drinking, and avoiding responsibilities. Extreme responses include alcoholism and drug abuse. People who engage in this type of behavior think they are making themselves feel better. Actually they are acting in a way that hurts them in the long run and does not help them deal with their troubles. When your troubles seem too difficult to manage, you might be considering one of these negative escape responses just to forget about everything. It is extremely important that you share these feelings with a trusted family member, friend, instructor, or adviser.

Winners know that living with less stress does not mean they will never feel anxious, worried, or tense. Everybody feels these emotions sometimes. Winners have simply learned how to balance the amount of tension in their lives. Pay attention to your body and mind, and look for patterns of behavior that create stressful feelings. Once you recognize certain negative behaviors, you are one step closer to changing them and replacing them with positive thoughts and actions.

No matter what your problems are, you can work on them in a way that is healthy and constructive. Depending on whether you are a racehorse or a turtle, you can choose the method that best fits your personality type. You can win.

Use Exercise.   Exercise can be a powerful stress reducer. Exercise includes walking, running, aerobics, or any other physical activity that helps you release tension. Deep breathing brings more oxygen to the brain and muscles. Exercise increases your heart rate and

Choose exercise or relaxation as an escape response to stress.

improves your circulation. Flexing muscles creates a massage effect and helps work out tension. Remember the "fight or flight" response that Dr. Waitley mentioned in his discussion of stress? Exercise helps to burn off the adrenaline that was released into the bloodstream.

Practice Relaxation. There are several ways you can achieve a relaxed state. A good way to deal with stress is through simple relaxation or meditation. Try sitting in a comfortable position in a quiet room. Focus your mind on a single calming word or phrase. Close your eyes; breathe deeply and slowly. Feel your muscles relax. Assume this calm attitude for about 20 minutes. Make time for a relaxation period every day, and you'll notice the difference in the way you feel both mentally and physically.

Another good way to relax is listen to music. Slow music is more soothing than fast music, and instrumental is more soothing than vocals. If you are very stressed, you may want to start with fast, loud music to match your mood and then gradually change to more mellow sounds. New Age music is very soothing, and there are also recordings available of sounds of nature. Some people relax to the sound of the ocean's surf, rain or thunderstorms, or birds and insects in a meadow.

Watching nature can be as relaxing as listening to nature. Try sitting in front of a fireplace or fish tank and lose yourself in watching the movement.

Take a Reality Check. Stop for a moment and try to step outside the situation. Ask yourself, "Am I overreacting?" How would you view the situation if it were happening to someone else? How do you think others are viewing your reaction? Ask yourself, "What is the worst thing that could happen?" Often you will realize that the situation isn't as bad as you first thought. With this new adjusted outlook, you can ease both your tension and your stress.

Laugh It Off. Look for the light side of a situation. If the situation doesn't seem to have a light side, read or watch something you find funny. Laughter affects the body in the same way that aerobic exercise does. It raises the blood pressure, heart rate, and muscle tension. Afterwards, a general muscular relaxation takes place.

Slow Your Thoughts Down. Take time to enjoy life, or as the saying goes, "Stop and smell the roses." On your hectic commute to school or work, look for beauty around you. You probably won't find it in the traffic, but look for beauty in a sunrise or sunset, trees and flowers budding in the spring, or leaves turning color in the fall. Take time to pay attention to and appreciate the world around you.

Dealing with Anger

Control your response to anger by staying calm and taking positive action.

Dr. Waitley spoke about anger and how we sometimes find ourselves getting upset with other people. Too often, people express their anger in self-defeating ways: they yell, throw tantrums, and might even strike someone. After such an outburst, though, do they feel better? No. A recent article in a health magazine discussed people who had frequent fits of rage. These angry individuals felt bad about themselves. They felt panicky and out of control, and the problems they were angry about still remained. Most of the time, our anger doesn't really help us. When we are angry, we feel helpless and frustrated. We would feel better if we used our energy to come up with solutions to the problem. Remember, you are responsible for your own anger. You can control it, and you can decide how you want to feel.

Sometimes we feel anger when people criticize us or disagree with us. This anger comes from our own negative thoughts. Other people cannot make us feel wrong or worthless. If we feel that way, it is because we have chosen to react that way.

It can be very difficult to keep a positive attitude when others around us are being negative. Some people think that if they make us feel bad, they'll feel better. It is important to remember, though, that no one can force you to be angry. When you choose to be angry, you have chosen to accept the negative influence of other people. It is a choice you have made. When we blame others for our negative emotions, we are only fooling ourselves.

There are two types of anger: that which we turn inward and that which we turn outward. Anger that we keep inside can make us resent people. We tend to feel guilty and depressed. Anger that we direct at others is often said to be "healthy" anger because we are openly expressing it. It is much healthier, though, to learn how to deal with others without anger. When we look at a problem calmly, we are closer to finding a solution.

Remember adrenaline? Anger is another trigger for your body to release both adrenaline and a stress hormone, cortisol. When these two hormones are working together in your body, your immune system may be weakened and unable to fight off disease. Redford Williams, M.D., a Duke University internist, says, "Every time you get angry it hurts your health."

We need to learn how to stop creating our anger. It is important to know when anger is an appropriate response to a situation.

When we stop and think about the situation, we develop our self-awareness and our feeling of control. We can decide how we will look at each situation.

Stay Calm.   For example, if after being put to bed your two-year-old comes walking out to see you while you're studying, you might have several reactions. One might be to become angry and say, "That child never stays put!" In your anger, you might yell at your child and then remain so upset you can't concentrate on your studies. Another reaction might be to think, "We both need to relax. I'll take a break and read a soothing bedtime story so we can spend a little time together." After you've put the child back in bed, you are still calm and in control and can go back to your assignment.

The way you choose to think about a situation often determines your feelings about it. Many situations can be a source of anger or stress because you see them in an unreal or exaggerated way. When you overreact to something, you are allowing yourself to be angry when anger isn't really necessary.

Take Positive Action.   It is easy to think that other people are causing all of our stress. However, it is possible that the problem lies in the way we are looking at others. Ask yourself these questions:

- Am I trying to change or control others?
- Am I prejudiced against this person? Am I too judgmental?
- Am I expecting too much from other people?
- Am I wanting people to be more like me?

People often get angry because they think their situations are unfair. Looking for fairness in every situation can be a fruitless search. It is important that we learn to accept things we cannot change. We can use our energy instead to change the things we can. How can you put this idea into action? Let's say you have to study for an exam on Monday and your house is always noisy on the weekend. Look at the situation in a realistic, practical way. If it is unlikely that you can find a quiet corner of the house to study in, make plans to study at the library. That is much easier than getting upset over the fact that your home is a lively, noisy one. You can choose not to create a stressful situation.

Creating Mental Self-Awareness

Make choices you feel comfortable with.

When you are honest with yourself, you are less likely to create stress. In his book *Seeds of Greatness*, Dr. Waitley offers a list of questions that can help you determine whether you are being honest with yourself when making a decision. You can ask yourself the following questions:

- Is this action what I believe I should do?
- Does what I say agree with what I do?
- What effect will this decision have on the other people involved?

Making a decision with these questions in mind will help you make the right choice with total self-honesty.

Journalist Linda Ellerbee advises doing what you believe is right. She refused to exploit victims of tragedy by interviewing them and instead found other ways to show the sadness of the situation. She says that if you go against what you believe is right, "You'll have the nagging feeling you knew all along it wasn't the right way to go."

Remembering that personal decisions affect other people is important to best-selling author John Grisham (*The Firm, The Pelican Brief, The Client*). He once said that he refused to write anything that might embarrass his mother or his children. Maria Shriver, a television journalist, once turned down an important interview with a foreign leader because she had promised to be with her daughter on her first day of preschool. The result? Two weeks later, the interview was rescheduled, and the foreign leader's staff all wanted to know how Shriver's daughter was adjusting to the new school.

When you are true to yourself, you feel comfortable with yourself. When you are comfortable with yourself, you can deal with the stresses of the outside world with calm and confidence.

S C E N E

2–2

K A R E N ' S   S T O R Y

Karen is more self-aware and self-confident.

Karen was nervous on the first day of school and had convinced herself that she was alone in her feelings and that she was different from everyone else. Fortunately, the instructor had each student introduce herself or himself at the beginning of the class. Karen was nervous, but to her surprise, she found that most of the other students felt the same way she did. She also realized that she had a head start over many of the others: She already had a job with an accounting firm and was familiar with much of the work she would be learning to do. Karen developed empathy for the other students who were not as fortunate as she.

Karen also realized that her first-day jitters and anger were really reactions to stress. One way she decided to overcome that was to become more environmentally aware of the campus. She studied maps to find her classrooms and always knew where they were before the first class.

She also practiced physical self-awareness. On days that she had evening classes, she would take a walk at lunchtime and then eat a meal that would give her plenty of energy for the rest of the day. She knew that she would only have time for a quick sandwich before class.

Karen also began to practice techniques to relieve her stress. As she became more mentally self-aware, she knew that what worked best for her was a few deep breaths and a quick step back from the situation. She would then realize she could handle whatever minor problem she was facing. Karen focused instead on the bigger picture: She was working toward her accounting degree, and she knew she could succeed.

"How funny!" thought Karen. "I was so nervous on the first day. I was starting to convince myself that going to school was a bad idea!" Now Karen is more self-aware (environmentally, physically, and mentally) and is more self-confident. Karen is on her way!

THOUGHT-PROVOKING QUESTIONS

1. Think about the last time you felt angry and then write about it. Was it last week? Yesterday? Today? Looking back at the situation, how could you have handled it differently? What other choices did you have besides feeling anger? What will you do the next time a similar situation occurs?

2. What is the difference between empathy and sympathy? How are they the same? Can you feel one without the other?

3. Why should you challenge your potential? If you are never satisfied with your achievements, won't you create unnecessary stress for yourself? Can you use mental self-awareness to avoid stress?

4. Think back to the discussion about "racehorses" and "turtles." Which one are you? Why do you think so? What about your friends? How might a "racehorse" and "turtle" react differently to standing in a long line? An unexpected power outage? Rush hour traffic? Taking three children grocery shopping? What are appropriate escape responses for each situation? Would those responses be different for each personality type? Is one way necessarily better than the other?

5. Are there times when you should resist change and other times when you should adapt to change? How do you know when to change and when to hold firmly to your own opinions and beliefs? Do you believe that something new is necessarily better? Give an example of something new that was not or is not better.

Increasing Self-Awareness

This activity is planned to make you more aware of yourself within your environments (home, school, work, and community). Self-awareness is important to your success. Knowing yourself and how you "operate" in the world around you also helps you control stress.

Instructions:

1. *Read each of the 24 items on the following list.*
2. *Decide whether the statement is not true, somewhat true, or very true.*
3. *Circle a number 1 (not true) to 10 (very true) to show how true the statement is for you.*

	Not True			Somewhat True				Very True		
1. I go to movies, restaurants, etc., with friends.	1	2	3	4	5	6	7	8	9	10
2. I spend time thinking positively.	1	2	3	4	5	6	7	8	9	10
3. I exercise each day.	1	2	3	4	5	6	7	8	9	10
4. I enjoy time with my spouse or a special friend.	1	2	3	4	5	6	7	8	9	10
5. I have set goals for earning and spending money.	1	2	3	4	5	6	7	8	9	10
6. I am satisfied with my career choice and my career progress so far.	1	2	3	4	5	6	7	8	9	10
7. I am involved in community affairs.	1	2	3	4	5	6	7	8	9	10
8. I enjoy reading books or magazines.	1	2	3	4	5	6	7	8	9	10
9. I belong to a club or social group.	1	2	3	4	5	6	7	8	9	10
10. I have set personal goals—certain things that I want to do and to be.	1	2	3	4	5	6	7	8	9	10
11. I eat healthful foods.	1	2	3	4	5	6	7	8	9	10
12. I write or call family members from whom I am separated.	1	2	3	4	5	6	7	8	9	10
13. I earn the income I want.	1	2	3	4	5	6	7	8	9	10

	Not True		Somewhat True			Very True		

14. I am involved in creative work—on the job or elsewhere.   1 2 3 4 5 6 7 8 9 10

15. I belong to a community association.   1 2 3 4 5 6 7 8 9 10

16. I attend workshops or special courses to increase my knowledge or skills.   1 2 3 4 5 6 7 8 9 10

17. I like to meet new people and to "hang out" or socialize.   1 2 3 4 5 6 7 8 9 10

18. I read books or take courses for the purpose of self-improvement.   1 2 3 4 5 6 7 8 9 10

19. I keep my weight under control; it's not more than 15 percent above the ideal weight for my gender, height, and age.   1 2 3 4 5 6 7 8 9 10

20. I have co-workers who are also friends.   1 2 3 4 5 6 7 8 9 10

21. I have a plan for saving money.   1 2 3 4 5 6 7 8 9 10

22. I have reached some, but not all, of my professional goals.   1 2 3 4 5 6 7 8 9 10

23. I volunteer from time to time for community projects.   1 2 3 4 5 6 7 8 9 10

24. I listen to audiocassette programs to learn more.   1 2 3 4 5 6 7 8 9 10

Instructions:

1. *Review the list and the circled numbers.*

2. *Put a ✶ in front of each item for which you circled 1–3.*

3. *Put a ✓ in front of each item for which you circled 4–6.*

4. *Examine the ✶ items. Where do most of the items fit—your home, school, work, or community environment?*   _____

5. *Look again at the ✓ items. In which environment do most of these items fit—home, school, work, or community?*   _____

6. *Refer to Step 4. List three things you could do within the next 24 hours to start making these "not true" statements true for you.*

    _____

    _____

    _____

⁊   *Refer to Step 5. Name three things you could do this week to make these "somewhat true" items "very true."*

    _____

-   _____

—   _____

Keep A   vity 2–1 for later use. Because it contains valuable information about you, you will want to   ne back to it often. It will help you, especially, with Activities 2–3 and 2–4.

Balanced Living

If you have not done Activity 2–1, Increasing Self-Awareness, please do so before starting this activity.

In Activity 2–1, you were asked to rate yourself in the main areas, or environments, of your life (home, school, work, and community). In this activity, you will look more closely at such areas. The purpose: to see if you devote about the same amount of time and attention to all areas (balanced living) or if you overlook one or more area (unbalanced living).

Taking a closer look means you must view your life in smaller parts than these four main areas. Besides home, school, job/career, and community, the list below includes attitude, health, money, recreation, and relationships—all important parts of who you are.

Instructions:

1. *Refer to Activity 2–1, Increasing Self-Awareness. For each of the 24 items on that list, write the rating you gave it (1–10) on the correct line below.*
   Example: Begin with the first item listed below, Item 2. Look up Item 2 on Activity 2–1, note the rating, and write that number on the line provided below. Repeat for the next item on the list.

Attitude		*Money*		*Community*		*Recreation*	
Item 2	_____	Item 5	_____	Item 7	_____	Item 1	_____
Item 10	_____	Item 13	_____	Item 15	_____	Item 9	_____
Item 18	_____	Item 21	_____	Item 23	_____	Item 17	_____
Total	_____	Total	_____	Total	_____	Total	_____

Health		*Relationships*		*Job/Career*		*School*	
Item 3	_____	Item 4	_____	Item 6	_____	Item 8	_____
Item 11	_____	Item 12	_____	Item 14	_____	Item 16	_____
Item 19	_____	Item 20	_____	Item 22	_____	Item 24	_____
Total	_____	Total	_____	Total	_____	Total	_____

2. *Add the ratings in each group and write the total.* _____

3. *In which area(s) of your life did you rate the highest?* _____

4. *In which area(s) of your life did you rate the lowest?* _____

5. *What do these ratings tell you about your priorities (what is important to you)?*

_____

_____

_____

Wheel of Life

On the Balanced Living exercise that you just completed (Activity 2–2), you added up the ratings from the self-awareness exercise for the primary areas of your life. Now you will create a Wheel of Life picture to help you see whether your life is "in balance."

Instructions:

1. *Record the total for each area in Activity 2–3 on the wheel below. Using the numbers on the spokes of the wheel as a guide, shade the section of the wheel to match each total.*

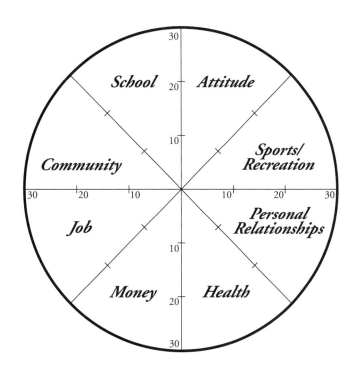

2. *What does your Wheel of Life look like? The more nearly perfect the circle shown by shaded areas, the more "in balance" your life is.*

3. *In which area(s) of your life do you want or need to spend more time?* _____

_____

4. *In which area(s) can you spend less time (to "make time" for the area written in Step 3)?*

    _____

5. *Name specific time wasters and/or involvements that you are able and willing to give up to increase*

    the balance in your life. _____

6. *Are you willing to state in writing (for your eyes only) your willingness to increase balance in your life? If so, you can fill in the blanks of the following statement and sign and date it.*

    I will spend less time   _____

    so that I can spend more time   _____.

    I will recheck my balance on *(write date about a month from today)* _____.

    Date: _____   Signed: _____

7. *Mark your calendar to redo these activities in about a month. Ask your instructor for a new copy of Increasing Self-Awareness, Balanced Living, and Wheel of Life.*

Stress Test

Stress is all around. Positive, or "good," stress, like a new job, feels good. Negative, or "bad," stress, such as the loss of someone close or an argument with someone at work, doesn't feel good at all—it hurts.

Stress, good or bad, affects how you think and how you act. The following list of thoughts and actions is planned to help you spot negative stress in your life. Use it to rate your stress level, that is, to see how stressful your life is.

Stress is personal, as you know from reading Chapter 2. So this stress test has no right or wrong answers—only *your* answers.

Instructions:

1. *Read each statement.*
2. *Decide how often the statement describes* you: *never, seldom, sometimes, or often.*
3. *Circle the number to the right that fits you.*

		Never	Seldom	Sometimes	Often
1.	I often lose my appetite or eat when I am not hungry.	1	2	3	4
2.	My decisions tend to be hasty rather than planned. I feel unsure about many of my choices and change my mind often.	1	2	3	4
3.	The muscles of my neck, back, or stomach frequently get tense.	1	2	3	4
4.	Thoughts and feelings about my problems run through my mind.	1	2	3	4
5.	I have a hard time getting to sleep, wake up often, or feel tired.	1	2	3	4
6.	I feel the urge to cry or to get away from my problems.	1	2	3	4
7.	I let anger build up and then "explode" in hostile, even harmful, ways.	1	2	3	4

	Never	Seldom	Sometimes	Often
8. I have jitters (nervous habits).	1	2	3	4
9. I feel tired, even when I have not been doing hard work.	1	2	3	4
10. I have physical problems, such as intestinal disorders or nausea.	1	2	3	4
11. I cannot do what I or others expect because the expectations are unreal or I have tried to do more than I can do.	1	2	3	4
12. I lose interest in sex.	1	2	3	4
13. I get angry easily and quickly.	1	2	3	4
14. I have bad dreams or nightmares.	1	2	3	4
15. I worry a lot.	1	2	3	4
16. I use more coffee, tobacco, alcohol, and/or drugs than I did a year ago.	1	2	3	4
17. I feel uneasy, without any reason that I can name.	1	2	3	4
18. When I talk, my words come out weak, fast, broken, or tense.	1	2	3	4
19. I am short-tempered and testy or cross with people.	1	2	3	4
20. Delays of any kind make me extremely impatient.	1	2	3	4

Rating Your Stress Level:

1. *Add up all of the circled numbers in each column.*
    Add those four subtotals together for a total stress score. _____

2. *Look up your stress level rating below:*

Rating	Level of Stress
20–40	Low level of stress
41–60	Moderate level of stress
61–80	High level of stress

3. *Read these paragraphs about what the rating means:*

This stress test is only a guide. A high (or low) rating may point to stress problems—or it may not. The rating partly depends upon how you interpreted the 20 statements.

Too much stress can mean problems; too little stress can also. If your stress rating is above 70 or below 30, and you are concerned about these results, you should see an adviser. A professional can evaluate other signs of stress that go beyond the range of this test.

Personal Stressors and Relievers

Stress is a natural, normal part of life. Everyone has to deal with it. Your stress comes in the everyday situations as well as the big events in your life. Your stress is not a direct result of the situations and events themselves, but of how you "see" or feel about them. For this reason, Dr. Waitley did not give you a list of stressors that every student can use.

This activity asks you to name current situations and events that you see as stressful. Before doing so, you should be aware of these points:

1. You are likely to feel stress when facing situations that make you change old ways of doing or thinking. Big changes usually bring on more stress than little ones, but a lot of small changes at one time can add up to become stressful. Starting college, marrying or divorcing, receiving a promotion, and losing a dear friend are examples of big changes. Moving to a new address, changing college programs, joining a fraternity or sorority, and working full-time instead of part-time are also examples of change that may cause you to feel stress.

2. You are likely to feel stress when asked to do a task for which you think you lack the needed resources, such as time, skill, knowledge, equipment, money, or moral support. Stress comes from uncertainty—not knowing for sure whether you can do what is asked. Stress comes also from not wanting to disappoint the person (instructor, boss, parent, etc.) who gave the assignment. Your stress is likely greater if the effect of not doing the task will be unpleasant for you (failing grade, warning or dismissal from job, disappointed or angry parent, etc.).

Instructions:

1. *In the left-hand column below, list situations and events in your life right now that you see as stressful. After listing a few, stop to think. Then, list more stressors. List all that come to mind.*

2. *In the right-hand column, list two or three ways you can relieve the stress. (Refer to Activity 2–1, Increasing Self-Awareness. The statements there may suggest some ways of relieving stress. You will not find all the "answers" in Activity 2–1, however.)*

Example:

Stressors	Stress Relievers
Too much homework; too little time.	I can do homework the same hours each day. I can get more sleep so I feel like doing homework. I can do some homework on weekends.

Stressors

Stress Relievers

_____   I can _____

I can _____

I can _____

_____   I can _____

I can _____

I can _____

_____   I can _____

I can _____

I can _____

_____   I can _____

I can _____

I can _____

_____   I can _____

I can _____

I can _____

_____   I can _____

I can _____

I can _____

_____   I can _____

I can _____

I can _____

_____   I can _____

I can _____

I can _____

Instructions:

3. *Draw a circle around the stressful situation (left-hand column) that bothers you most right now.*

4. *Look at the "I can" statements you wrote for this stressor. In the following space, write a promise, an "I will" statement.*

To relieve some of my stress, by the end of today I will _____

_____

_____

_____.

5. *Sign the pledge you made to you:* _____

6. *Write reminders where you will see them often:*

    a. *Remind yourself daily to stick to your signed promise.*

    b. *Remind yourself to come back to this page in a few days to write "I will" statements for the other stressors listed. (Write these statements on notebook paper or a card that you can carry with you.)*

The words "I am . . ." are powerful words—be careful what you hitch them to.

A. L. Kitchman

3

Psychology of Self-Image

After you read this chapter and complete the activities, you will:

- Understand how you form your self-image in your subconscious mind.

- See how you can change your self-image by changing your attitude and behavior.

- Develop your self-image to see yourself as you really are, regardless of what others may say.

- Be able to use your imagination and creativity to visualize success.

S C E N E

3–1

P A U L ' S   S T O R Y

"What if I'm not smart enough?"

Ever since Paul was a little boy, he has loved animals. He had many pets as he was growing up and was always taking care of stray animals.

Although Paul had once dreamed of being a veterinarian, he gave up that dream in high school. His family couldn't afford to send him to college, and his grades weren't high enough to earn a scholarship. Neither of Paul's parents had gone to college, and they didn't believe that he should either.

Paul was able to earn enough money to enroll in a veterinary assisting program. If he couldn't be a vet, at least he would be able to work for one.

Paul's sister would often make fun of him. She would say that Paul couldn't be a doctor and he couldn't be a vet either. She said Paul was so stupid he'd be lucky if the vet would let him clean the kennels. Why pay a school to learn to do that? He should just get a job.

Paul was looking forward to his future career but was overwhelmed with all the course work. There was so much to remember! All these complicated terms. And why did he have to pass another math class? After getting low grades on his last two quizzes, Paul began to wonder if his sister was right. Maybe he wasn't smart enough and this *would* be a waste of time and money.

Paul was ready to quit but thought about making an appointment with his adviser.

If you were in Paul's situation, would you seek help?

Dr. Waitley discusses the principle of self-image by focusing on the conscious and subconscious mind, different factors that contribute to your self-image, and how to use your imagination to change your self-image.

What Is Self-Image?

Your self-image is the mental picture you have of yourself.

Self-image is the way we see ourselves in our minds. How we see ourselves is very important, for everything that we will ever try to do is based on the image we have our ourselves. It is as if we each have a videotape in our minds that contains hundreds of millions of pictures of ourselves. We have collected these pictures over the years. All these pictures together make up our self-image.

The History of Your Self-Image

The beliefs we have about ourselves were formed in the past. All our experiences, successes, failures, embarrassments, victories, and relationships with others have helped to shape our self-images. Once this image is planted in our brains, we see it as being completely true. We don't ask ourselves whether our self-image is false or not. We accept it as the absolute truth, without asking questions.

Self-images were developed in our past but affect our future.

Each of us, from the beginning of childhood, weaves a fine web of self-images that grows from our ideas, our parents' comments to us, and the comments of our teachers and friends. These self-images begin as flimsy cobwebs that become stronger over time, like steel cables. They can support us and make us strong, or they can weigh us down like a ball and chain. All self-images can be changed, though. The power of suggestion, as we will see, can have a very strong effect on us. Remember: It's not what you are that holds you back, it's what you think you are.

Blue-Eyed, Brown-Eyed

A positive self-image creates the potential to succeed.

A teacher once conducted an experiment on the students in her class, with their parents' consent. The teacher told the class that scientists had found that people with blue eyes have greater natural learning abilities than people with brown eyes. She then divided the class into two groups, those with blue eyes and those with brown eyes. She had them wear signs that said "blue eyes" or "brown eyes." After a week, the grades of the brown eyes fell significantly while the level of the blue eyes improved. The teacher then made a startling announcement to the class. She had made a mistake! It was the blue-eyed people who were weaker students and the brown-eyed who were smarter. Up went the grades of the brown-eyed students and down went the performance of the blue-eyed students. Talk about the power of suggestion!

Self-Defeating Attitudes

The student who sees herself as an "F" student will often receive that grade. The new employee who has an image of himself as unpopular may find it hard to make friends. People with a negative self-image develop a **self-defeating attitude** in which they see themselves failing before they even try. They reinforce this self-defeating attitude through negative self-talk: "I'll probably flunk this test," or "I know I won't be invited to go out with everyone after work."

A self-defeating attitude will sabotage your chances for success.

This type of negative thinking can invite rejection. We have all noticed people at a social gathering who look uncomfortable, self-conscious, or maybe a little hostile. Why would anyone want to approach such persons? They may think they want to attract people, but they really are driving everyone away. Negative thinkers need to encourage themselves to put on friendly smiles or to introduce themselves to others.

You are your own greatest critic. You can hurt your self-image with critical remarks, or you can build yourself up to reach the sky by giving yourself praise, encouragement, and a pat on the back.

Labels

A big part of our self-image consists of **labels**: statements we use to define who we are. The problem with labels is that they can be very limiting, and often are not even true. Labels tend to be negative. Yet people get so attached to the labels they have given themselves (or other people) that they can't let go. If you can't let go of those labels, you can't begin to change your self-image. We often say things like the following:

"I'm a lousy cook; I can't even boil an egg."
"I can't dance."

"I have a poor sense of humor."
"I have a terrible memory."
"I'm never on time."
"I have bad luck."

Each of us is controlled by these pictures we have formed in our minds. We cannot outgrow the old limits we have placed on ourselves in the past. We can only set new ones.

Winners develop positive labels to reinforce positive self-images.

Winners develop and actively think about a healthy self-image. Winners act like Winners. They imagine—with pictures, feelings, and words—the roles they want to play. They give themselves a kind of preview of coming attractions. Winners might describe themselves as follows:

"I like to cook appetizing meals."
"I'm a pretty good dancer."
"I have a fine sense of humor."
"My memory is dependable."
"I'm usually early for appointments."
"I'm a lucky person."

Imagination

Every living organism has a built-in guide to help it achieve its goals. Animals have a basic instinct to find food and shelter, run from or fight enemies, and reproduce to keep their species going.

You are a unique gift of creation. Your imagination of your possibilities will set the limits on what you do with yourself. Human beings have emotional and spiritual needs that other animals do not. Humans also have a "success instinct" that is different from anything animals possess. They have the ability to imagine things that can happen in the future.

Winners use their imaginations to create successful situations.

Human beings are more than creatures, they are creators. They can create their own success by using their imaginations, by forming a mental image of what they want. The French emperor Napoleon once said, "Imagination rules the world." One hundred years later, the famous thinker Albert Einstein corrected him. "Imagination is the world," he stated. The world you picture in your mind is the world in which you really live.

Use your imagination to win!

Your Subconscious Mind

Your subconscious mind controls your attitudes and your personality.

We have both a conscious and a subconscious mind. Our **conscious mind** controls sensations and emotions. It collects information from our environment, stores it in our memory, and helps us make logical decisions. Our **subconscious mind** stores the emotions and sensations that we are not quite aware of, the feelings that are just under the surface. Many of the thoughts and attitudes that help make up our self-image are subconscious ones.

Attitude is the first step in achieving something. If you have the attitude that you will be successful at something, you are well on your way to achieving that success.

The "truth" you feel about yourself will control many of your everyday decisions. This "truth" may be just a figment of your imagination shaded by the environment around you. This is your subconscious at work.

If you try to change something about yourself at the conscious level, using will power, the change will usually be only temporary. Let's say you have been a pack-a-day smoker for many years and decide to give it up. You tell your conscious mind that you are quitting smoking. Then your subconscious mind remembers all the times you have tried to quit in the past and asks your self-image for a report. Your self-image is that of a smoker, so your conscious mind tells you that you are a smoker who will fall back into the habit one day soon.

If you want to make a permanent change in your personality, you must first change your self-image and your lifestyle. Then your long-range behavior will follow. Your behavior, personality, and achievement are all a part of your self-image.

A Winning Self-Image

Winners control their self-images and change them when they desire. They realize that it takes days and weeks of taking ideas and turning them into reality to create a better self-image. It takes discipline and dedication to totally change your image from the inside.

Positive self-images are created—they don't just happen.

Winners know that worry, anger, and depression can destroy their creative imaginations. Winners always think about the self-image of that person they would like to become. They get a clear picture of themselves as if they had already achieved their goal. Winners tell themselves over and over again that they are winning each personal victory now. A world-champion figure skater once said, "I rarely fall because I practice each sequence in my imagination with my eyes closed and could successfully perform my routine blindfolded."

Your dreams, daydreams, and imagination can shape your destiny. Winners play "Let's Pretend"—they make believe they are where they want to be. They make believe they are already the persons they want to become. They visualize achieving the goals they have set. Winners like Michael Jordan and Jackie Joyner-Kersee can hear the roar of the crowd. They can feel the solid gold medals around their necks. They can visualize what they want to achieve and make it happen.

Winners feel like Winners. Winners "see" through the eyes of Winners. What can you see for yourself? What do you want to do tomorrow? Who do you want to be tomorrow? Think Win!

Let's take a closer look at some of the points Dr. Waitley discussed and learn how to use the principle of self-image in our everyday lives.

The Importance of a Positive Self-Image

Your self-image can control your success or failure.

Your self-image is the way you see yourself and what you think others see in you. A positive self-image is seeing yourself as someone worthy of reaching goals and achieving success. You see yourself as someone who deserves happiness. You can't move toward your goals until you believe deep down that you deserve them. A positive self-image helps form the basis of a winning attitude.

Dr. Waitley and others have explored the principle of self-image by conducting surveys, interviewing people, and observing human behavior in different situations. Dr. Waitley tells us that people can be their own best friends or worst enemies. They can build themselves up or tear themselves down.

Creating Your Self-Image

Your self-image is the end result of many things. All your memories and experiences, as well as your reactions to them, combine to form a picture of yourself in your mind. Your own thoughts, as well as the thoughts and opinions of others, feed your self-image.

In his book *Who Do You Think You Are?* Joel Wells remarks that often "our self-image is . . . dictated by others, put together over the years in bits and pieces. Parents, childhood playmates and school-mates, teachers, relatives, athletic coaches, friends, fellow workers, bosses, ministers, priests, and rabbis all contribute."

We should take the responsibility to create the self-image we wish to have. Then we can allow the people in our lives to have a positive or negative effect on that self-image. Encouragement by our friends and family, instructors, and co-workers strengthens our healthy self-image. Do we think we are nice just because other people tell us so? No. We think we are nice—or smart, or athletic—because that is the vision we have of ourselves. We let others' good opinions feed that image. When people are not supportive and encouraging, does that mean we have lost our good qualities? Not at all. We must, however, ignore those opinions that might hurt our self-image.

Accept only positive reinforcements to your self-image.

For example, if your classmate makes a comment about your low test grade, does that make you a poor student? No! You can still see yourself as the same hardworking student you were when you walked into the room. People's opinions don't change who you are. It is your responsibility to see that they don't change who you think you are.

Searching for Identity

Accepting negative labels can limit your potential.

Many people feel unsure of themselves and who they are. They search for a self-image and an identity. They search for a place in life. Other people may give them labels such as pretty or ugly, smart or dumb, popular or unpopular. All of us tend to compare ourselves to others and form a self-image based on these comparisons: "She makes more money than I do," or "He's smarter than I am." These self-images, formed early, often stay with us in our subconscious minds.

Whenever you hear yourself thinking negatively, stop and really think about your attitude. As Jon Kabat-Zinn says, "Whatever has happened to you, it has already happened. The important question is, how are you going to handle it?" You may not be able to control some of the events in your life, but you can control your reactions to them. Strive to think of a glass as half full rather than half empty.

Our self-image determines how we present ourselves to the world. It affects what we think we can accomplish professionally. It affects our choices in personal and professional relationships. A poor self-image often means low self-esteem. A positive physical image helps us think in a positive way. When we look in the mirror and see a happy, attractive person, we feel good about ourselves. Attractiveness has very little to do with "good looks" and everything to do with a positive, cheerful attitude.

When all else fails, look into the mirror and smile as if you were greeting a friend you haven't seen for awhile. A genuine smile can bring a boost to anyone's day.

Ideals

What forces outside us help create the image we have of ourselves? The images that we see in the movies, on TV, and in magazines tell us we should look a certain way, dress a certain way, or drive a certain car. We then believe that if we look like the models in the ads, we will be rich and charming, and everyone will like us. The problem is that we feel like fakes when we try to be like someone we are not. We are not being true to ourselves. It is not the real us but an **ideal,** or an image we think we should have.

Do not use unrealistic expectations as goals.

People trying to live up to some ideal of beauty can lead unhappy and even unhealthy lives. For example, for many years, it was fashionable for women to have very small waists. So to become fashionable, women wore heavy corsets under their clothes. These corsets, which were often made of wood, whalebone, and sometimes even steel, were tied very tightly. They were tied so tightly that it was extremely difficult to breathe in them. Women wearing corsets could do little but sit down. They were too short of breath to walk or run. Some women suffered damage to their internal organs because of the pressure from the corset. This might sound to you like an old-fashioned, out-of-date example. You can probably think of many ways in which people today are willing to suffer discomfort and even pain to be fashionable. Everyone likes to look good and wear nice clothes, but Winners know that they don't have to suffer pain in order to look good. They can look great and be comfortable, too.

In a 1984 study, 33,000 women were asked about their weight and their self-image. Seventy-five percent of the women said they felt fat, even though only about 25 percent of them were actually overweight. Another survey, done in 1990, found that only 19 percent of the women questioned liked the way their bodies looked.

Although more women than men are concerned with thinness, both sexes feel pressure to look a certain way. Of course, there is nothing at all wrong in wanting to look good. Having pride in your appearance is a sign of a positive self-image. The danger is that many people begin to equate their sense of self-worth with their appearance and forget that a positive self-image is not so much about how you look as about who you are. A positive self-image should be concerned with a healthy body rather than a specific target weight.

☞ *Developing Your Creativity*

As Dr. Waitley mentioned, your creativity and imagination affect your self-image. Creativity gives you a willingness to see the possibilities in life. It gives you the tools to create possibilities where it seems none exist. There are several questions you can ask yourself to measure your creativity:

- Am I hopeful about the future?
- Do I want to change things?
- Am I curious?
- Am I open to new ideas?
- Am I willing to take risks?
- Do I think for myself?

If you answered yes to many or all of these questions, you are likely to be a creative person. You are interested in the world around you and eager to open your eyes to new experiences.

Self-Image and Creativity

An open, positive self-image increases creativity.

In his book *A Whack on the Side of the Head,* author Roger von Oech described the problem of a major oil company. The top executives in the company were concerned about the lack of creativity among some of their "idea people"—those whose job it was to come up with new ideas in research and development. The management hired a psychologist to figure out why some employees were very creative while others were not. The psychologist asked the employees many questions about themselves. After three months of study, the psychologist came to the conclusion that the successful, creative people had positive self-images; they thought of themselves as creative and spoke of themselves that way; the less successful people did not.

Obviously, your self-image has a big effect on how you go through life. It has a big effect on your professional and personal relationships. The way you view yourself has an effect on your actual performance and achievements. It stands to reason, then, that the way to start improving your life is to start working on your self-image.

Visualization

One of the first steps in developing a positive self-image is to visualize yourself in a positive way. Visualizing your desired self-image will help you to achieve it. In his book *The Seven Habits of Highly Effective People,* Stephen R. Covey says that **visualization** is the ability to see success, feel success, and experience success before actually completing the activity. Visualization is using your imagination in a very positive way.

A positive self-image helped famous children's author Madeleine L'Engle get through a difficult time. At one point in her career, L'Engle, who had already published several books, found that publishers were turning down her books and she could not get them into print. One day, after she had received yet another rejection notice, she put a cover over her typewriter as a sign that she was finished with writing forever.

Then she thought, "I am a writer. That is who I am, even if I am never published again." Her positive image of herself was clear. Though her next book was turned down about 30 times, she never gave up. It was finally accepted by a publisher and went on to sell millions of copies.

Dr. Waitley agrees that, to achieve the positive self-image you want, it is helpful to visualize yourself as the person you want to be. It is important to do this every day. Visualize that all the changes you want to make are taking place—right now. Visualize that you are the person you want to be—right now. Visualization is not about wishful thinking, it is about confidence and positive thinking.

Use visualization to create a successful attitude.

In a situation where you would usually say "I can't" or "I won't be able to," you must instead visualize yourself succeeding. Take a few deep breaths to help yourself relax. Then, in your mind, visualize or imagine yourself succeeding in the situation. Repeat the scene over and over again until you truly believe that you will be able to succeed in the situation.

For example, let's say that as you are studying there is something you don't understand, but you feel uncomfortable asking questions in class. Right now phrase your question and visualize yourself raising your hand. See the instructor call on you and visualize yourself confidently saying, "Could you please explain more about . . . " or "Could you please explain how to . . . " The key is to visualize your self-confidence. When you have the opportunity in class to ask your question, you will have had experience—if only in your mind—of asking it with confidence.

A strong, positive self-image can be your greatest asset in going after what you want in life. Visualize yourself as a successful student. When you really see yourself getting the grades you want and getting the diploma, certificate, or degree you want, you will have taken the first step toward achieving that goal.

It takes patience and hard work to replace a poor self-image with a healthy one, but it is worth the effort. Every day that you visualize your new, positive self, you are that much closer to achieving that goal and all the goals in your future. Picture yourself as a Winner!

S C E N E

3–2

⌒

P A U L ' S   S T O R Y

Paul chooses a new self-image.

Paul's adviser talked with Paul about his decision to quit school. Paul explained the trouble he was having in class and the things his sister was saying about him.

Then Paul's adviser asked why he had enrolled in the course. Paul explained why he had thought he wanted to be a veterinary assistant, and he became very enthused as he was talking about his love for animals and his past experiences in nursing sick animals back to health.

From their conversation, Paul began to see that he had developed a self-defeating attitude and had accepted the negative labels his sister had given him. He also learned that he had the power to change his attitude.

With some help from his adviser, Paul learned some visualization techniques that gave him confidence in himself and his abilities. He knew that it would be hard work to pass his classes, but he also knew that he was capable of doing so. Whenever he felt down and ready to give up, he visualized himself in a vet's office helping make the visit a pleasant one for both the pet and its owner. He heard the person say, "I'm always so glad when you're here to help us. You always make this trip an easier one. Thank you for being so caring."

That was just the boost Paul needed to study a little harder
for that next quiz!

THOUGHT-PROVOKING QUESTIONS

1. Think about the following saying: "It is not what you are that holds you back, it is what you think you are." What do you think this means exactly? Do you agree with this statement?

2. How do our past experiences shape our self-images? Write about an early experience in your life that helped to shape the way you feel about yourself today. Can two people sharing a common experience develop different self-images?

3. How can positive and negative feelings you have about yourself affect the way others look at you? How can negative and positive feelings others have toward you affect your own self-image?

4. How can we tell the difference between a positive self-image and an unrealistic ideal? Can you use your self-awareness to help tell the difference?

5. Think back to the example of women wearing corsets to fulfill an unrealistic and unhealthy ideal. What are some other ways that people are willing to suffer discomfort and pain to strive for an ideal?

Imagine That . . .

In this activity, you are asked to relax and dream. Five scenes are described below, and you are to picture yourself in each one of them.

_____

Instructions:

1. *Imagine yourself in Scene 1. Notice details of your dream picture. Jot down key words on the lines provided if it will help you see the details of your vision. When does this scene take place? (What year? What season? What time of day?) Where does the scene occur? (Describe the place to yourself.) Who is with you to share the experience? (How many people? Who are they? How do they look? What do they say to you?) What are you doing and saying? How do you feel?*

    Scene 1: You have been recognized by your employer at a meeting of your co-workers for outstanding work. You are being promoted; you start your higher-level job the first of next month.

    When _____

    Where _____

    Who _____

    What _____

    Feelings _____

2. *Repeat Step 1 for Scenes 2 through 5.*

    Scene 2: You are enjoying a happy time with your family at your favorite spot for rest and relaxation.

    When _____

    Where _____

    Who _____

    What _____

    Feelings _____

    Scene 3: You are experiencing a personal victory. For a long time you told yourself, "I think I can." Then, "I know I can." Now you can say, "I did it! I knew I could."

When _____

Where _____

Who _____

What _____

Feelings _____

Scene 4: You have just received a big paycheck, including a bonus, and have put the money to good use.

When _____

Where _____

Who _____

What _____

Feelings _____

Scene 5: Someone you care about is enjoying a personal victory of her or his own.

When _____

Where _____

Who _____

What _____

Feelings _____

3. *Create a scene of your own; repeat Step 1.*

Scene 6: _____

_____

_____

When _____

Where _____

Who _____

What _____

Feelings _____

The Pen Pal

Instructions:

1. *Describe yourself in a letter to a man or woman you have never met. You cannot enclose a photograph, so you will have to use words to paint a picture of yourself. Describe your appearance (height, hair color, etc.) but don't stop there. Describe the way you walk, talk, and laugh. What does your voice sound like? Is there a celebrity who looks like you?*

2. *Take a few minutes to imagine the person you are writing to. (Give him/her a name: _____*.)*

   Plan your letter by writing key words here: _____
   _____

3. *Write the letter in this space:*

_____

(Today's date)

Dear *_____

_____

_____

_____

_____

_____

_____

_____

_____

_____

_____

Cordially

_____

(Your Name)

4. *Imagine you have an identical twin, who looks, talks, and acts just as you do. Write another letter. This time, though, describe your twin. Use this space to plan (write key words):*

_____

_____

_____

5. *Write the "twin" letter:*

_____
(Today's date)

Dear * _____

_____

_____

_____

_____

_____

_____

_____

_____

_____

Cordially

_____
(Your Name)

6. *Look at the two letters. How are they different? Did you describe the same features in different ways?*

_____

_____

7. *How do you explain these differences (listed in Step 6)?* _____

_____

_____

_____

Admire a Hero

If you think back to early childhood, you may recall a person who was your hero, perhaps a parent or an older sibling. As your world became larger, you found other heroes besides those at home. Perhaps you admired your teacher, a sports figure, or someone you read about in a book at school.

Adults have heroes too, of course. Some heroes are noted for special achievements in their particular fields. Others are noted for feats of courage or generosity or honor.

Maybe you have noticed that as an adult—just as in the past—you tend to imitate in your life the traits you admire about your hero. That person serves as a model, or role model, of the person you want to become. Studying your heroes and thinking about why you admire them is a good way to build your own self-esteem.

Instructions:

Read a biography of someone you admire. When you finish reading, think about the person's story for a day or two. Then fill in the answers below.

Name of hero: _____

Date of birth: _____

Job/Title: _____

Person's main accomplishments: _____

_____

Problem(s) person overcame: _____

_____

What you admire about him or her: _____

Traits that you and he or she have in common: _____

_____

Qualities he or she has that you would like to have:_____

_____

Ways person may have acquired these qualities: _____

_____

Dream Job

Like Activity 3–1, this activity involves your ability to imagine, to project your thoughts to a future time and another place.

You will complete a job application form for the job of your dreams. On this application, though, you won't write past accomplishments and present qualifications. Instead, you will apply for your dream job 10 years in the future, listing what you expect to achieve and what you'll be able to do then.

Before you apply for a job, you need a description of it. Since only you can describe your dream job, space is provided for you to do just that.

Instructions:

1. *Ten years from now, the calendar will show what year?* _____ *(Use this year on your job description and application form.)*

2. *Describe your dream job, using this job description form.*

DREAMON INC
Job Description

Job title: _____

Department: _____

Supervisor: _____

Date: _____

Job summary: _____

_____

Job duties: _____

_____

Working conditions: _____

_____

Required to qualify: _____

_____

---

3. *Refer to the job description and fill in the unshaded sections of the job application form on p. 69. Remember, you are NOT limited to the knowledge, skills, and traits you have now. Think in terms of your potential—the person you can become. (Be sure to sign your dream job application.)*

4. *Today is (circle one):   M   T   W   Th   F   Sa   Su.   On this day next week, take out the application form and read it again. Do the same the next week and the next. . . . As you work toward your goal, you may want to make changes on the form. Do so!*

5. *Recommendations: Keep the application private at first. Later, share it with only those persons who believe in and support you.*

APPLICATION FOR DREAM JOB
Please print in ink   AN EQUAL OPPORTUNITY EMPLOYER

NAME (LAST, FIRST, MIDDLE INITIAL)	SOCIAL SECURITY NUMBER	DATE

ADDRESS (NUMBER, STREET, CITY STATE ZIP CODE	U.S. CITIZEN? YES NO

HOME PHONE #	REACH PHONE #	FAX # AND/OR E-MAIL ADDRESS	DATE YOU CAN START

ARE YOU EMPLOYED NOW?	IF SO, MAY WE TALK WITH YOUR EMPLOYER?

TYPE OF WORK DESIRED	REFERRED BY	SALARY DESIRED

IF RELATED TO ANYONE IN OUR EMPLOY, STATE NAME AND POSITION

DO YOU HAVE A PHYSICAL CONDITION THAT MAY KEEP YOU FROM DOING CERTAIN KINDS OF WORK?   YES   NO   IF YES, EXPLAIN

HAVE YOU EVER BEEN CONVICTED OF A FELONY?   YES   NO   IF YES, EXPLAIN

E D U C A T I O N	INSTITUTION	LOCATION (CITY, STATE)	DATES ATTENDED FROM	TO	DIPLOMA/DEGREE/ CREDITS EARNED	MAJOR SUBJECTS

LIST BELOW THE POSITIONS THAT YOU HAVE HELD (LAST POSITION FIRST)   CONTINUE ON BACK IF NECESSARY.

1. NAME AND ADDRESS OF FIRM	DESCRIBE POSITION
EMPLOYED (MO/YR) FROM: TO:	REASON FOR LEAVING
2. NAME AND ADDRESS OF FIRM	DESCRIBE POSITION
EMPLOYED (MO/YR) FROM: TO:	REASON FOR LEAVING
3 NAME AND ADDRESS OF FIRM	DESCRIBE POSITION
EMPLOYED (MO/YR) FROM: TO:	REASON FOR LEAVING

I UNDERSTAND THAT I SHALL NOT BECOME AN EMPLOYEE UNTIL I HAVE SIGNED AN EMPLOYMENT AGREEMENT WITH THE FINAL APPROVAL OF THE EMPLOYER AND THAT SUCH EMPLOYMENT WILL BE SUBJECT TO VERIFICATION OF PREVIOUS EMPLOYMENT, DATA PROVIDED IN THIS APPLICATION, ANY RELATED DOCUMENTS, OR RESUME. I KNOW THAT A REPORT MAY BE MADE THAT WILL INCLUDE INFORMATION CONCERNING ANY FACTOR THE EMPLOYER MIGHT FIND RELEVANT TO THE POSITION FOR WHICH I AM APPLYING, AND THAT I CAN MAKE A WRITTEN REQUEST FOR ADDITIONAL INFORMATION AS TO THE NATURE AND SCOPE OF THE REPORT IF ONE IS MADE.

SIGNATURE OF APPLICANT _____

Admire Me

A past activity pointed out that we all have people we admire. Activity 3–3 caused you to think about the people you respect: parents, instructors, friends, historical figures, talented athletes, entertainers, political figures, and so on.

You also have admirable qualities! Keys to self-esteem include (1) recognizing those qualities in yourself and (2) appreciating them. What do you admire about yourself?

Instructions:

1. *List some of your admirable qualities by answering these questions: What do I like about me? If other people were asked to list my admirable qualities, what would they put down?*

_____ _____ _____

_____ _____ _____

_____ _____ _____

_____ _____ _____

_____ _____ _____

2. *Pause about two minutes and think more about your characteristics. Add to the list in Step 1. (You may continue on a separate sheet of paper if you need more space.)*

3. *What terrific things did you discover about yourself? In the list, put a star (*✳*) beside one quality you were not aware of at the beginning of this activity.*

4. *Check (✓) the quality you believe is your strongest one. This probably is a trait you have been developing for a long time.*

5. *Circle a trait you would like to make stronger.*

6. *Using your responses in Steps 3–5, write a summary of your admirable qualities. Suggestion: Begin by stating the fact that you have admirable qualities; follow with a few examples. Then finish the summary.*

We are all born into the world with nothing. Everything we acquire after that is profit.

⌒

Sam Ewing

4

Psychology of Self-Esteem

After you read this chapter and complete the activities, you will:

- Know why it is an important step to success to build your self-esteem.

- Be able to identify behaviors associated with both low and high self-esteem.

- Be able to recognize some self-defeating barriers that block positive self-esteem.

- Be able to identify some steps to build high self-esteem.

- Be able to list some characteristics of winners with high self-esteem.

S C E N E

4–1

S A R A H ' S   S T O R Y

"Have I made the right decision?"

Sarah was undergoing many changes in her life. She was 33 years old with two children in high school. Sarah's husband had recently been killed in a car accident by a drunk driver, leaving Sarah as the sole support of the family. Her husband had insurance that paid for his funeral and would give Sarah enough to pay the bills for a year while she went back to school.

Because Sarah had dropped out of high school, married young, and had a family, she really had no skills for a good-paying job that would support her family at the same level that her husband had.

After thinking about her interests and abilities, Sarah decided that she should pursue a career in fashion merchandising. She was always being complimented on her choice of clothing, and even her daughter's friends asked for her help. As the first week of classes came to an end, though, Sarah began having second thoughts about her decision to go back to school.

"Look at all these kids; I feel so old," she said to herself. "And it's been so long since I studied math and English and everything else. It seemed so much easier when I helped my kids with their homework. What if I fail all my classes? I was never a great student. But if I quit now, what else can I do? What would my family do?

I don't think I could get a job that would pay all the bills. Maybe I should quit school and get two jobs—one during the day and a part-time job at night."

Do you think Sarah should go back to school?

Dr. Waitley looks at Self-Esteem and suggests ideas on developing high self-esteem and practicing positive self-talk.

What Is Self-Esteem?

The word *esteem* means to appreciate the value or worth of something. **Self-esteem** is confidence and satisfaction in yourself. High self-esteem is accepting yourself the way you are at this moment. It means using logical thinking, not emotion, to power your actions and decisions. Self-esteem is one of the most important basic qualities of a winning human being. It is that deep-down, inside-the-skin feeling of your own worth that frees you to achieve your goals for job success and personal happiness.

Winners like themselves.

"I like myself. I really do like myself. I'm glad I'm me. I'd rather be me than anyone else living now or at any other time in history." This is the self-talk of a Winner, and healthy self-talk is important to developing self-esteem. Winners develop strong senses of self-worth and self-confidence.

Learning to Like Yourself

Some people are born with a lot going for them at the start. Many children have been encouraged by winning parents, outstanding teachers, coaches, and friends who gave them early feelings of self-esteem. This is probably the most important quality of a good parent or a good business leader: giving positive encouragement to help others develop a positive self-worth.

Winners build their own self-esteem.

Not all Winners were born feeling good about themselves. Often, they had to learn to like themselves through practice. Self-esteem comes from inside. It comes from having confidence, and confidence comes from succeeding. Often when we begin something new, we have little confidence because we have not yet learned from experience that we can succeed at it.

Some people from poor or unhappy backgrounds have become outstanding Winners. Basketball star Isiah Thomas came from a background of poverty and hardship but developed high self-esteem. He gave himself goals to shoot for. Sometimes you work harder to get those things that aren't handed to you.

A Lifetime Program

As we were growing up, most of us were told what to do and what not to do by adults. "Don't interrupt," "Children should be seen and not heard," "You're not old enough to do that!" or "You should know that by now." Sometimes this kind of talk creates troubled teenagers. It can divide children and parents, students and teachers.

Winners continue to develop their self-esteem all through their lives.

As we grow to adulthood, these messages can cause us to walk a tightrope between humility and humiliation. Humiliation is a feeling of extreme shame. It happens when we are embarrassed or criticized too much. **Humility**, on the other hand, can be a positive trait and means we can accept it when someone corrects us and we can learn from our errors. Winners learn that self-development is a lifetime program.

Self-Worth

Some people are easily hurt by the words and actions of others. Often, these people have very low self-esteem. People with low self-esteem value others' opinions and judgments more than they value their own. When others' judgments are negative, people with low self-esteem tend to be more hurt and upset than people with healthy self-esteem. They feel undeserving, doubt their own abilities, and have a poor opinion of themselves. People who suffer from low self-esteem place a very low value on their own worth. On the other hand, individuals with high self-esteem know they are important, valuable people. They have confidence in themselves.

Winners value their own opinions.

Focusing on Success

Many times, when we begin something new, we have very little confidence in ourselves. For example, when you learned to drive a car, you didn't know if you would be successful until you tried. Sometimes it takes a lot of trying to achieve success, but when we finally do, we feel confident. We have learned again that we can succeed at something new.

Winners learn from mistakes and remember successes.

Winners focus on past successes and forget past failures. They learn from their mistakes and then erase them from memory. Winners know that it doesn't matter how many times they have failed in the past. Instead, they remember and dwell on their successes.

We may often find we are comparing ourselves to others, but it's important that we learn to look only at our own abilities, interests, and goals. We should think logically, not emotionally, about what actions to take and decisions to make. Emotions are automatic, subconscious reactions. Winners enjoy their emotions but base their decisions on logic and common sense. Relationships are stronger when they are entered into intelligently as well as emotionally.

Winners accept themselves—even though they're not perfect.

To develop high self-esteem, we need to take pleasure in where we are, instead of always thinking the grass is greener somewhere else. Winners accept themselves as they are at this moment, with whatever weaknesses they may have. Since the perfect human being has not yet been discovered, we need to live with our problems until we can work to change them. An important part of self-esteem is **self-acceptance**—living your life as it is unfolding. It means accepting all responsibility for what happens in your life.

Self-Talk

To develop self-esteem, it's important to practice positive **self-talk**. This means telling your subconscious mind that you are doing fine. The spoken word has a powerful effect on our bodies as well as our minds. Thoughts can raise and lower body temperature, relax muscles and nerves, raise and lower pulse rate, and more. So we need to control the language we use when we talk to ourselves. Instead of saying, "I can't" or "I wish," Winners say:

> "I can."
> "Next time I'll get it right."
> "I look forward to . . . "
> "I'm feeling better about . . . "

Winners accept a compliment with a simple "Thank you."

A good way to measure someone's self-esteem is to notice the way he or she accepts a compliment. Someone says: "Your oral report was really good." A person with low self-esteem might say, "James's report was better." A person with high self-esteem would probably say, "Thank you." Accepting compliments lets others know you accept your own value and the value others place on you.

Winners in sports, business, education, or any other activity in life accept their own uniqueness. They feel comfortable with their images and are willing to have others know them and accept them just as they are. Winners naturally attract friends and supporters. They seldom have to stand alone.

Not all Winners received the gift of self-esteem from their parents. Many had to pull themselves up and develop their own high standards. Winners are aware of their great potential and like who they are. Since they have a deep feeling of their own worth, they are eager to love others as they do themselves. High self-esteem—it's one of the most important qualities of a Winner. Talk yourself up!

Let's take a closer look at some of the points Dr. Waitley discussed and learn how to use the principle of self-esteem in our everyday lives.

The Importance of Self-Esteem

Self-esteem is having confidence in your ability to deal with the challenges of life. It is believing that you are worthy and deserving of success. Self-esteem is the fuel that takes you on your drive toward your dreams.

Studying Self-Esteem

In 1990, California created a task force to study self-esteem. The final study defined self-esteem as "Appreciating [my] own worth and importance, and having the character to be accountable for [myself] and to act responsibly toward others." According to the California report, people with high self-esteem tend to be less involved in negative behaviors such as drug and alcohol abuse, crime, child abuse, and educational failure.

People with high self-esteem are less likely to participate in negative behaviors.

A 1992 Gallup Poll interviewed 612 adults about their feelings on self-esteem. When asked how important self-esteem is in motivating a person to work hard and succeed, 89 percent answered, "Very important."

We are always trying to understand more about self-esteem and its importance to us. There have been more than a thousand scientific studies done on self-esteem, and researchers have tried to measure it with 200 different tests. Most of the tests ask people to agree or disagree with statements such as "I am happy with myself." Nobody is certain that we can accurately measure self-esteem, but most people agree on its importance.

Low Self-Esteem

Low self-esteem can lead people to spend time trying to run away from pain. As Freud observed, low self-esteem creates a feeling that says, "I can't do anything." People with low self-esteem find it hard

People with low self-esteem tend to seek negative escape responses.

to value themselves. They think they are worthless and that their lives will always be unhappy. Unfortunately, people who suffer from low self-esteem often turn to drugs or alcohol to escape their negative feelings. Such escape responses, of course, do not solve problems but only add to them.

Confronting problems head-on might seem like a very painful thing to do, but it's the only way to solve them. And, with the support of family and friends, it might not be so painful after all.

High Self-Esteem

High self-esteem helps us survive the challenges of day-to-day life. It helps give us the strength to deal with everyday problems and stressful situations. The more you build up your self-esteem, the less you see yourself as a victim of chance. Instead, you can start to see yourself as a strong person who can deal with any situation.

People with high self-esteem tend to make positive choices.

High self-esteem can help you make positive decisions at school. If a certain field of study interests you, feeling good about yourself can encourage you to push ahead and take on the challenge of learning something new. It can help you decide to sit up straight in the front row, ready to participate and learn, rather than hoping to blend in somewhere in the back of the classroom.

☞ Feeling Good about Others, Too

Psychologists agree that high self-esteem is a good goal to work toward. More and more, experts are pointing out that when you feel good about yourself, you tend to feel good about others, too. When you value yourself, you value others as well and treat them in a respectful and responsible way.

If you like yourself, you will be able to like others.

This does not mean, however, that you should let other people's opinions determine your self-esteem. It is risky to connect your feelings of self-esteem to anything or anyone outside yourself. Other people's choices or actions should not affect your feelings about your own abilities and potential. We know that self-esteem actually means being the best "you" possible, not rating your success in comparison to others'. You can be successful along with everyone around you. You can also be successful if no one around you is a success. When you feel good about yourself, you are a success!

It is also important to know that we must set goals to please ourselves, not other people. If you set your goals to please other people,

Set your goals to please yourself.

you will end up doing what others want, rather than what you want. Psychologist Ellis reminds us that it is not necessary to be loved by everyone for everything you do. By trying to please everyone, you may find that you please no one at all, including yourself.

Studies have shown that people with high self-esteem go after their goals. They are not roadblocked by people or circumstances. They tend to go after more demanding jobs, which challenge them and at which they will have to work hard. They don't settle for jobs that do not satisfy them.

Some experts believe that the personality and characteristics we are born with have much to do with self-esteem. Interestingly, though, some people who are raised in an "ideal" environment with much praise and love may grow into insecure adults who are unhappy in their lives. Others, who grew up in the worst conditions, can mature and find high self-esteem and success. No matter what kind of environment we come from, we can value ourselves and work to create new environments that are worthy of us.

Building Your Self-Esteem

Each person must accept the responsibility for building a positive self-esteem. To do this, you need to know how to overcome common barriers, deal with past failures but build on past successes, and create a support system to help you with your efforts.

Recognizing and Overcoming Barriers to Positive Self-Esteem

Before you can improve your self-esteem, you must identify some self-defeating ways of thinking. Once you are aware of a specific problem or behavior, you can work to overcome it. The key is to take a negative outlook and change it to a positive one.

Imagine that you have planned a picnic for a group of friends. You've reserved a shelter house in a public park. The sky is filled with clouds on the morning of the picnic. Two hours before the picnic, it begins to rain. At picnic time, the rain lets up to a light drizzle. The temperature, however, is warm, and all of your friends come to the picnic. Almost everyone makes some wisecrack to you about the weather and the fact that you were "in charge." Think about how you feel about yourself. Do any of the following describe you?

Do you react to disappointments with negative or positive responses?

Accepting personal responsibility for all problems.   Do you accept the blame for choosing the day it rains? "It's my fault we had the picnic today. I should have had it yesterday; the weather was beautiful then. I'm sorry." Or do you realize that no one can control the weather? Don't blame yourself for the weather—or anything that you can't control.

Exaggerating problems.   Do you think the entire day is ruined and dwell only on the rain? "This is terrible! Everyone and everything will get soaked! We can't even roast marshmallows over an open fire! This is the worst picnic ever. We should just cancel altogether and everyone go home." Or do you realize that a little drizzle won't really hurt anyone? Step back and do a reality check so the problem doesn't seem bigger than it actually is.

Having an egocentric outlook.   Do you think the world revolves around you and your problems? "I have the worst luck! No matter what I do, it goes wrong! It would have to rain on the day of my picnic." Or do you realize that it is also raining on every other outdoor event planned that day? Remember that you aren't the only one affected by the circumstances.

Having a limited outlook.   Do you think there are only two sides to every situation—a winning side and a losing side? "Well, we can stay here and have a terrible time, or we can cancel and everyone can go home." Or do you look for alternatives and make the best of the situation? Instead of football, you might play charades instead. Don't limit your options in any situation; always look for new opportunities.

Imagining the worst.   Do you think that all is lost because of this one "failure"? "The day is ruined. My friends won't like me anymore. They think I'm incompetent." Or do you realize that nothing has really changed in your friendships? Do you realize that this one event won't ruin your entire future? The worst rarely happens. Give yourself a break, and don't dwell on negative thoughts.

Letting the situation overwhelm you.   Do you see yourself as helpless? "There's nothing I can do. Everything is ruined. Nothing can go as planned." Or do you tackle each small obstacle and come up with a simple solution or alternative? Are you thankful that you reserved the shelter so that everyone can get out of the rain? Can you improvise garbage-bag raincoats for all your friends? Instead of a hot dog roast, can you have cold cut sandwiches? Joan Lunden, co-host of *Good Morning America,* has taken to heart a quote from Jon Kabat-Zinn's *Wherever You Go, There You Are* that would apply here: "You can't stop the waves, but you can learn to surf."

Developing Strategies to Improve Self-Esteem

Take positive steps to build your self-esteem.

When you have made the decision to build your self-esteem, it won't just happen. You must start somewhere to *make* it happen. Congratulate yourself for taking the first step—making the decision to think better of yourself. In *Who Do You Think You Are?* author Joe Wells lists some positive steps you can take to build your self-esteem:

- Get healthy. To feel good about yourself, you first need to feel good physically.
- Think about your strong points.
- Congratulate yourself. Tell yourself, "Great job!" and "Only you could have pulled that off!" Recognize your efforts.
- Get involved, be a volunteer. You can take pride in helping others.
- Specialize in something. Make yourself really good at something that interests you.

These are steps toward both building your self-esteem and maintaining it. Once you take these steps, continue them throughout your life.

Remembering Past Success and Forgetting Past Failure

Having high self-esteem also means that you don't think of yourself as a failure just because you have had a failed experience. We know that being human means making mistakes. Winners know that a failure is an event, not a person. The failure is actually a tool for you to use. It is feedback that lets you know where to work to improve.

You may fail an exam in school. That does not mean you are a failure. It simply means you failed one exam. With the right study skills and habits, you may do better on the next exam. That one failure does not define who you are. Winners look at failures as opportunities to do better next time. Winners remember the exams in the past on which they had been successful.

Try to repeat your successes and learn from your failures.

Actor and comedian Jim Carrey was heckled in his first try at comedy and didn't try again for two years. He says, "I have no idea what motivated me to try again. I just felt like giving it a shot. Failure isn't the end unless you give up."

Feeling bad after a failure is normal and understandable. It isn't realistic to think we can force ourselves to feel good all the time. Sometimes we feel good, and sometimes we feel bad. Instead of trying to change our feelings, it does us more good to try to fix the problem. When we start to work on solving the problem, we may find that our mood has improved all by itself.

Creating a Personal Support System

How else can we build our self-esteem? One way to build self-esteem is to develop a strong support system: a group of people we can go to when we need to talk about a problem. The people in our support system help and encourage us. Your support system might include parents, brothers, sisters, spouses, instructors, religious leaders, neighbors, and friends.

Support others, and they will support you.

Sometimes your support system might include an adviser, for those times when you need extra support in dealing with a problem. In turn, you will probably find yourself part of someone else's support system and be able to listen and encourage him or her when that person has a problem. Many people find that helping others increases their own self-esteem, and they pursue some kind of volunteer work on a regular basis.

Signs of Self-Worth

What does a person with high self-esteem look like? Nathaniel Branden lists some ways in which that feeling of self-worth shows through. When someone enjoys high self-esteem:

- He can talk honestly about his achievements or shortcomings.
- She feels comfortable giving or getting compliments and expressing affection.
- He is open to criticism and can admit mistakes.
- She is open to new ideas and experiences.
- He has a good sense of humor.
- She can stand up for herself.
- He handles stress well.

One of the most important elements of high self-esteem is self-acceptance. It's great to want to improve yourself, to be that special person you want to be. The real key to self-esteem, though, is to like and value yourself even before those goals are reached. Self-esteem is knowing that you're special now.

S C E N E

4–2

S A R A H ' S   S T O R Y

Sarah builds up her self-esteem.

Sarah was doubting her decision to return to school after having been away for many years. She told her neighbor, Keisha, that she felt silly going to school with students who were so much younger and that she'd decided to quit.

"But you can do it. Your family is so proud of you!" Keisha said. "Of course it isn't easy, but you're working toward your goal! Don't give up on your dreams again."

"Yeah, Mom," said her son. "You were going to get your degree and work in a big department store. Who cares if you're older? I bet you're a lot smarter." Her daughter reminded her how much her friends appreciated her advice when it came to fashion.

The more she talked with her friends and family, the better Sarah felt. So what if she was a little bit older than the other students? She was going to think instead about her new career and the new life she was going to make for her family. Sarah's family, her personal support system, was proud of her.

Sarah realized that she was facing a few barriers to building up her self-esteem. Once she identified the fact that she was exaggerating her problems, imagining the worst, and letting the situation overwhelm her, she was able to work on positive thoughts to improve her self-esteem.

Sarah decided to forget her past failures; she had learned that quitting school wasn't the right answer. Then Sarah began to remember some of her past successes. Even though her part-time jobs had been low-paying, she had always been a reliable, dependable employee. In fact, several employers had told her that she would be able to move "up the job ladder" if she went back to school for more education and training.

As Sarah began developing her new positive outlook, she was also developing good self-esteem and a sense of confidence in her ability to achieve her goals.

1. Why do you think we sometimes tend to focus more on our failures than our successes? Is it easier to put things in perspective when you're talking about a friend's failures? Why do you think that's so? Why do you think we tend to judge ourselves more harshly than we judge others? How can we learn to be easier on ourselves?

2. Charles Osgood, star of CBS News's *Sunday Morning Show,* once said, "I realized I shouldn't try to be like anyone else. The only thing I was good at was being Charlie Osgood." Which principle was he applying?

3. One way to establish high self-esteem is to focus your attention on your successes and good experiences. Write about a recent success you have had that made you feel good about yourself. Explain how your accomplishment raised your self-esteem.

4. You can build high self-esteem by learning from past mistakes: looking back at an unsuccessful project and using the knowledge you gained in a helpful way. Do you know someone who has been able to turn a failed situation into a useful learning experience? What did he or she learn?

5. Often, when someone is very critical of others, it is said that the person has low self-esteem. Why would low self-esteem cause the person to act that way?

Test Your Self-Esteem

You've read about self-esteem. You have a general idea what self-esteem is and how to build it and keep it—in spite of occasional failure. Again and again, Chapter 4 noted the importance of positive self-esteem to success (that is, successful people, or Winners, like themselves). Now is a good time for you to measure your self-esteem. Activity 4–1 is designed to do just that. Remember that this activity is *not* a measure of your value but an indicator of how much you value yourself.

Instructions:

For each of the 20 items below, use a pencil to circle the letter (a, b, or c) of the statement that best describes you.

1. a. I don't care if people say bad things about me. Sometimes, I even like it when someone is bothered by what I do or say.
   b. My feelings are hurt if someone disapproves of me or of what I do or say.
   c. When someone criticizes me, it increases my caring about or understanding of that person.

2. a. I feel I'm able to control what people do or how they feel. I seem to need that control.
   b. Too often, I feel out of control or powerless, or I feel manipulated.
   c. I am in control of myself. No one can control me, and I don't want to control anyone else.

3. a. I think of myself as being better than other people.
   b. I think of myself as being less important than other people.
   c. I'm no better or less important than anyone else.

4. a. How I look is very important to me. I always want to look my best and to be in fashion.
   b. I don't care much about the way I look as long as I'm comfortable.
   c. How I look is important because it shows how I feel about myself. I keep myself in good shape.

5. a. I don't mind a good argument. It helps to clear the air and makes life more interesting.
   b. I dislike fighting or arguing, and I'll do whatever I possibly can to avoid it.
   c. I don't try to avoid arguments; they're all right with me. Still, I don't try to win them at the other person's expense.

6. a. I don't really care about helping other people. I easily turn down most requests for help.
   b. It's almost impossible for me to turn down a request for help.
   c. I help others but not if it means harming myself. I may turn people down when they ask for help.

7. a. I believe, or others tell me, that I'm a perfectionist. I'm not likely to be satisfied until things are done and done well.
    b. Often, I don't care if everything gets done or how well it's done. It just isn't important to me.
    c. Just about everything I do is done well. If not, I'm rarely bothered by it for very long.

8. a. I dislike making mistakes and avoid them whenever possible.
    b. Too often, my life seems to be filled with mistakes. I don't seem to be able to avoid them for long.
    c. I don't try to make mistakes; but when I do make them, I'm not bothered much or for very long.

9. a. I try not to ask for help. I feel I should be able to do without it.
    b. I don't mind asking for help, but often I don't get the help I really need.
    c. I usually know when I need help, and I'll ask for it until I get what I need.

10. a. I regularly criticize other people and situations. It makes me feel better to let out my feelings.
    b. I was taught it isn't right to criticize, so I avoid criticism as much as I can.
    c. I'm rarely critical. My mind simply doesn't work that way.

11. a. If someone disagrees with me, I think she or he has a different opinion. That's all right with me.
    b. If someone challenges what I believe is true, I'm likely to assume I'm wrong.
    c. If someone challenges what I believe is true, I usually think she or he is wrong, and I want to persuade her or him to think my way.

12. a. I'm comfortable with praise, but I don't really need it to feel good about myself and what I do.
    b. I need the recognition of praise for what I've accomplished.
    c. I don't much care if I get praised or not. In fact, praise often makes me feel uncomfortable.

13. a. I don't usually pay attention to who does or doesn't like me or how many friends I have.
    b. Few people like me. The ones who do like me are not people I care about.
    c. I like to have many friends. Keeping those relationships is very important to me.

14. a. Material wealth or professional success comes to me as a result of living my life happily.
    b. I don't much care about getting ahead in life. It would just mean having more to keep up with and to worry about.
    c. Getting ahead in life—achieving success or owning valuable things—is important to me, and I'm working hard for it.

15. a. I'm normally too busy enjoying or learning from what's going on to think or talk about past accomplishments.
    b. I don't have much to be proud of. Even when I do, I keep it to myself because a person shouldn't brag.
    c. I tell others about my successes and the good things that happen to me. I'm not shy about singing my own praises.

16. a. I'm entirely responsible for what happens in my life. Blaming other people or circumstances doesn't make any more sense than feeling bad about the past.
    b. Many of the bad things that happen in my life are my fault. I tend to feel guilty about or regret such mistakes.
    c. If something goes wrong, it usually isn't my fault. Other people or circumstances are more often to blame.

17. a. I have a positive sense of direction that comes more from my worth as a person than from the goals I set and attain.
    b. My life lacks direction. I have trouble imagining my situation getting better.
    c. I set goals and evaluate my progress in attaining them. When life gets tough, I think how good it will be someday.

18. a. I'm usually happy. When necessary, I speak up for myself without being harsh.
    b. I'm usually reserved. I always try to be considerate, even if it means my needs go unmet. I don't like to confront people.
    c. I'm outspoken and sometimes come across to others as aggressive. I have a manner that could be described as blunt or brusque.

19. a. People do what is in their interest whether it's fair or not. That's not wrong; it's just how people are.
    b. Most people look out for themselves and do whatever they can get away with. It's not right, but it's how people are.
    c. I have definite beliefs about what is and isn't fair. I'm upset when I am or other people are treated unfairly.

20. a. I know that what others say will not hurt me—only what I say.
    b. I try to be careful about what I say because I might hurt someone's feelings.
    c. I try to be careful about what I say because someone else might use it to hurt me.

21. On the scale below, circle the number that indicates how you feel about yourself right now.

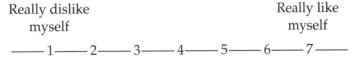

Really dislike myself   Really like myself

—— 1 —— 2 —— 3 —— 4 —— 5 —— 6 —— 7 ——

1. Go back to number 11. Beginning with this item and continuing through number 20, change each A you circled to a C; change each C to an A.

2. Add up the total number of A's, B's, and C's; record the numbers in the spaces provided.

    A's _____   B's _____   C's _____

3. Use the following information to interpret the numbers.

_____

Surface self-esteem:

What you think of yourself consciously. The number you circled in Item 21 represents your surface self-esteem.

Score Item 21	Interpretation
1–3	You need to work on your surface self-esteem.
4	Your self-esteem is about average.
5–7	Your surface self-esteem is good. Note: You still may need to work on your secret self-esteem. Scoring for Items 1–20 will tell you.

Secret self-esteem:

What you think of yourself subconsciously ("deep down"). The more C's you circled, the higher your secret self-esteem.

Score Items 1–20	Interpretation
11–20 C's	You honestly like yourself.
0–10 C's	Perhaps your secret self-esteem needs attention. Here is more information to help you do that.
8 or more A's	You tend to be critical of yourself and others. You need recognition and like to "get ahead." (These patterns are often attempts to hide a person's low self-esteem.) Work on your secret self-esteem to prevent building up too much stress. These patterns are called aggressive.
7 or more B's	You appear less forward, or pushy, and perfectionist than most people, but under the surface you are critical of yourself. You don't always speak up for your rights, and you tend to dwell on past failures. Your constant level of stress may be hurting your health, career, or relationships. These patterns are called passive.
Near equal number of A's and B's	You still need to work on your secret self-esteem, although you're neither very aggressive nor very passive.

Your Values

This activity will cause you to think about your values, that is, what's important to you, what gives meaning and purpose to your life. Noticing what matters to you is a way to build your self-esteem. When you name areas of your life that matter more than other areas, you are affirming your own worth, or value. Perhaps you've heard the expression, "It takes one to know one." Indeed, your ability to identify worth proves that you are worthy.

If you compare what matters most to you with other people's values, you are likely to find that you don't all value the same things. This discovery helps you see yourself as unique (one of a kind). In other words, no one can take your place; the world would not be the same without your special contributions to it.

Instructions:

1. *Rank the following areas of your life in order of importance to you, using the numbers 1 through 8 (1 = highest; 8 = lowest). Do not be too concerned if you have trouble deciding in some areas. Just complete the ranking.*

Area of Life	Ranking	Comments
Career	_____	_____
		_____
Church	_____	_____
		_____
Family	_____	_____
		_____
Friends	_____	_____
		_____
Health	_____	_____
		_____
Money	_____	_____
		_____

Area of Life	Ranking	Comments
School	_____	_____
		_____
Other (specify):		
_____	_____	_____
		_____

2. Go back over the list and explain why (Comments column) you ranked the area as you did.

3. Write a short message for your instructor stating which areas you ranked 1, 2, 3, and 8. (Use a separate sheet.) Also, explain briefly why you ranked these items as you did.

4. Share your rankings with another student in the class. One of you says what is ranked highest and why; then the other person does the same. Repeat this procedure for at least the first four items before skipping to the lowest ranked item on each list.

5. In what ways is the other person's list similar to yours? _____

    _____

    _____

6. How do the two lists differ? _____

    _____

    _____

7. How do you feel about your values (your rankings on this list)? _____

    _____

    _____

8. Check here if this activity helped you. * _____

    *Turn to Activity 7–1 at the end of Chapter 7. Place a check in the box there as a reminder to rank your values again later.

Do You Resist Change?

Building high self-esteem often involves change. Being open to changing negative things about yourself is the first step toward achieving healthier self-esteem.

_____

Instructions:

1. *Read the paragraph below about a group of people unwilling to change.*

   Members of a tribe in South America were dying for an unknown reason. Scientists went to visit the tribe and saw that they built their homes from a claylike mixture called adobe. After studying the tribe's surroundings, the scientists discovered that an insect living inside the adobe walls of the homes was biting the tribe members, poisoning and killing them. The scientists told the tribe members that they should think about how to stop the deaths. They could try to kill the insects, tear down the homes and build new ones, or move to a new location. The tribe said they would not move but would stay in their deadly insect-infested homes and take their chances. They continued to die off one by one.

2. *Answer these questions about this story.*

   a. For what reasons do you think the tribe members refused to move? Name as many reasons as possible.

   _____   _____   _____

   _____   _____   _____

   _____   _____   _____

   _____   _____   _____

   b. Which of the listed reasons is/are easiest for you to defend? Explain. _____

   _____

   _____

   c. What would you do in the tribe's situation or a similar one? _____

   _____

   _____

d.   Should everyone be open to change? Why or why not? _____

_____

_____

_____

e.   Should a person be open to change in every area of life? Why or why not? _____

_____

_____

_____

f.   Have you ever resisted change, even when it might have been good for you? If so, describe the situation in a paragraph like the one you just read.

_____

_____

_____

_____

_____

_____

g.   Is your ability to change related to your values (Activity 4–2)? If so, how? _____

_____

_____

_____

_____

h.   Why do you think you resist change, even change that would be good for you?

_____

_____

_____

_____

_____

3. *In the list below, check the actions that seem appropriate when you are facing a big change.*

_____ a. Decide in advance how much you are willing to change and how fast.

_____ b. Talk about the change and how it may affect you with someone who has made a similar change.

_____ c. Write down the "little things" in your life that may be affected by the "big change."

_____ d. Determine at least two good reasons why the change is not right for you.

_____ e. Prepare for the change like an actor preparing for a movie or play.

_____ f. Ask questions; be sure you understand why the change is necessary.

_____ g. If the change requires new knowledge or skills, read widely, take a course, or ask someone to coach you.

_____ h. Speak up to defend your rights with the person beginning the change.

_____ i. Sit calmly and picture yourself after the change.

_____ j. Keep a diary of the change, noting both the advantages and disadvantages to you.

_____ k. Make a list of problems caused by the change and go over it about once a week.

_____ l. Plan a strategy for getting out of the changing situation.

_____ m. Recall other changes you've made and how the situations turned out.

_____ n. Go with the flow; adjust as much as you have to but don't overdo it.

_____ o. Work out a way to keep as many of your old ways as you can while going along with the change.

_____ p. Recall your accomplishments before the change.

_____ q. If others are affected by the change too, get together with them to share your feelings about it.

_____ r. Expect stress to result from the change and choose techniques for dealing with it.

_____ s. Forget it; "this too will pass."

_____ t. Think more about the unchanged areas of your life.

_____ u. Keep a diary that you can review the next time you go through a big change.

_____ v. Talk with the people close to you about how they can help you during this change.

Positive Self-Talk

Someone has said, "When you talk to yourself, be careful what you say." Indeed, as Dr. Waitley noted, words have power to change you. Words can lift you up or put you down—whether you or someone else talks to you. Talking to yourself (self-talk), about yourself, with words that cheer and encourage you, is a good way to build self-esteem.

Zig Ziglar, noted author and speaker, advises people in his seminars to use positive self-talk regularly and often. In his book *Over the Top*, he gives the following two-step example.[1]

Step 1: Write this statement on an index card:

> I, (name), am an honest, intelligent, responsible, organized, goal-setting, committed individual whose priorities are firmly in place. I am a focused, disciplined, enthusiastic, positive-thinking, decisive extra-miler who is a competent, energized, self-starting team player determined to develop and use all of these leadership qualities in my personal, family, and business life. These are the qualities of the Winner I was born to be.

Step 2: Read this statement two or more times each day. Stand in front of a mirror, if possible and practical, looking yourself in the eye as you read it.

Instructions:

1. *Write a self-talk statement on a separate sheet or 3" x 5" card, following the Ziglar example. Follow these guidelines in creating your statement:*

    a. Include your name at the beginning of the statement.

    b. Write one or more "I am" statements.

    c. Use at least six positive words to describe yourself in the first sentence.

    d. Use additional positive descriptors in the next sentence. Here you may want to include a trait that you're working to improve. If, for example, you put things off and often miss deadlines, the statement may say, "I am disciplined and manage time well. I plan ahead and allow 'just-in-case' time. I am dependable and reliable; people can count on me to meet deadlines."

    e. Vary the statement to suit your style. For example, Ziglar gave another example that included these words: "I take genuine pride in my appearance. . . . My self-image is good and is getting better because I am. . . . "[2]

Activity 4–4 *(concluded)*

2. *Decide which of the following uses of your self-talk statement will work best for you:*

    a. Tape it to the mirror and read it aloud (quiet voice) first thing after rising each morning and last thing before retiring each night.

    b. Carry the card in your pocket or purse; take out the card three or four times each day and read it (aloud if possible).

3. *Start today. (Write today's date: _____) Repeat this action every day for the next 30 days. (Write the date in 30 days: _____) Expect your self-esteem to go up before the 30 days elapse, however.*

4. *After 30 days, write a new statement, involving another trait that you want to improve. Repeat Steps 1–3 continuously. Positive self-talk will always be effective, even if you use it every day for the rest of your life.*

[1]Zig Ziglar, *Over the Top* (The Zig Ziglar Corporation, 1994), p. 27.
[2]Ziglar, p. 61.

U-Turns Allowed

You are constantly talking—either to others or to yourself. You think in words, and your life is affected by this mental dialogue. While positive self-talk builds your self-esteem (Activity 4–4), negative thoughts about yourself lock up your brain power, your attitudes, and your actions.

Instructions:

1. *In the following list of negative self-talk statements, mark the statements that you say. Use these marks:*

O	=	Often say this statement.
S	=	Sometimes say this statement.
N	=	Never say this statement.

    _____   There aren't enough hours in the day.

    _____   I don't know where to begin.

    _____   Someday I'll get around to . . .

    _____   I'm no good at this.

    _____   I just don't know.

    _____   I blew it again!

    _____   If only . . .

    _____   I don't feel good.

    _____   I have to . . .

    _____   I can't help it.

    _____   I'm not up to it.

    _____   I don't think it'll work for me.

    _____   I have a terrible memory.

    _____   This looks really bad on me.

    _____   It's the same old grind.

_____ This place is a mess.

_____ I'll never get recognized.

_____ There's too much to do.

_____ It always happens to me.

_____ With my luck, . . .

_____ It's going to be one of those days.

_____ I've had it!

_____ I'm always the last to know.

_____ I give up!

_____ She (or he) always gets the breaks.

_____ I can't get along with people.

_____ Everybody gives me their work to do.

_____ There's no place to go with this dead-end job.

_____ I'm afraid . . .

_____ I wish . . .

_____ I can't decide . . .

_____ I'll never make it.

_____ I'm worried . . .

_____ That's just the way I am.

_____ I can't remember people's names.

2. *Copy each statement marked with O (Step 1) on the lines marked – (negative) below.*

– _____

+ _____

– _____

+ _____

– _____

+_____

−_____

+_____

−_____

+_____

−_____

+_____

3. *Change each example of negative self-talk (Step 2) to a positive statement. Put each positive state-*
    ment on the lines marked + (positive) above. Examples:

    −   I can't remember people's names.
    +   I remember people's names because I have a good memory.

    −   I don't feel good.
    +   My eating and sleeping habits, plus exercise, explain why I'm so healthy.

4. *Try to catch yourself the next time you engage in negative self-talk. Stop! Can you turn it around?*
    In the next three days, list a negative example each day. Then, show how you turned it into positive
    self-talk.

    Day 1

    −_____

    +_____

    Day 2

    −_____

    +_____

    Day 3

    −_____

    +_____

5. *Use this esteem-building activity (Step 4) all the time with the positive self-talk statement you cre-*
    ated in Activity 4–4. The power of words may surprise you.

The truth of the matter is that you always know the right thing to do. The hard part is doing it.

General H. Norman Schwarzkopf

5

Psychology of Self-Discipline

CHAPTER OBJECTIVES

After you read this chapter and complete the activities, you will:

- Practice self-discipline to try to make the most of each moment.

- Use self-talk to begin to break bad habits and replace them with new ones.

- Accept responsibility for your own actions.

- Succeed first in your imagination and then in reality.

- Keep moving forward, a little at a time, even when things get difficult.

- Seek support from others to help you achieve your goals.

S C E N E

5–1

R I C K ' S   S T O R Y

"Where do I begin?"

Paris! Rome! Madrid! Rick had always wanted to travel. Ah,
that would be the life—always headed to new exciting places.
Rick didn't know when he'd be able to visit any of those places;
he didn't even have a passport. What he did have were obligations.
He was 25 years old, divorced, and paying child support. He needed
to get a steady job and wanted one that would interest him and
make it fun to go to work.

Rick decided to be a travel agent and was working toward getting
his certificate. Since travel had always interested him, he figured
learning about it in career school would be easy. Now he was
starting to think he had gotten more than he bargained for. He had
gotten by in high school—why was career school so hard? Rick
was beginning to realize that whatever had gotten him through
high school wouldn't be enough to earn him a certificate in Travel
and Tourism. He was learning about geography, computerized
systems, and many other new things. Rick had a lot of work to do
and didn't know where to begin.

"Time to study for another exam," he complained to himself.
"Exams, homework, classes, reading—I didn't know career school
would be this much work! Why can't they just tell me about airline
ticketing and reservations and how to book hotels? I don't need to

know all this other stuff. I don't have enough time to read this chapter, do these assignments, and study for the English test on Tuesday. I have to be at work at 5 o'clock and I have a million other things to do. I don't want to spend all my time studying. Besides, how am I supposed to find the time to do everything? Forget it—I'll just look over the material during my break or maybe tomorrow on the subway or the bus."

What can Rick do to find time for all the tasks he needs to complete?

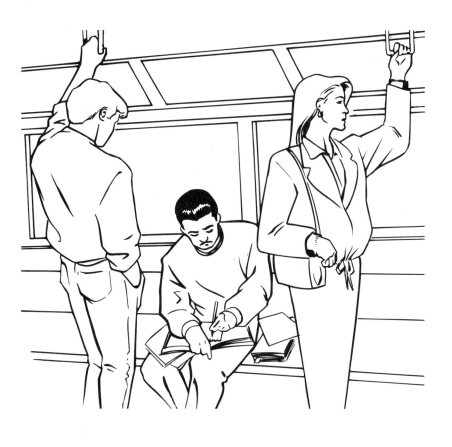

Dr. Waitley views self-discipline as a means to setting goals, breaking bad habits and replacing them with good ones, and changing one's self-image.

What Is Self-Discipline?

Self-discipline is teaching ourselves to do the things that are necessary to reach our goals, without becoming sidetracked by bad habits. A **habit** is a behavior we have developed by repeating it over and over. Habits are attitudes that become a part of our subconscious mind and can control our everyday lives. We can spend most of our time practicing our bad habits rather than trying to replace them with good ones. Habits may start off quite weak, but they soon grow strong and can be very difficult to break. The first step in breaking a bad habit is desire—we have to want to change.

The Desire to Change

Desire is a powerful emotion that helps you make plans and reach goals. Desire can help motivate you and give you a feeling of control. You might desire to fly to the moon—you might even imagine yourself on the moon—but in reality, you will never even get near the launching pad without self-discipline.

Winners desire to create new habits, goals, and images.

    There is a lot of effort involved in self-discipline. You have been the way you are for some time now, and every day your actions and reactions reinforce your self-image. You talk to yourself every minute you are awake to maintain who you are today, and you have done this every day of your life. Self-discipline is committing to memory all the new thoughts and emotions that you want to replace the information you have stored in your memory bank. By constantly repeating these new thoughts, by self-talk or imagination, you will cause them to take root in your subconscious. The result is a new habit, goal, or self-image.

See the Experience

All the Winners you will ever meet in life can picture or visualize each experience they want, each goal they want to achieve, and each habit they want to change. They place the picture in their subconscious minds and "print" it in their brains. They use self-discipline to tell themselves over and over with words, pictures, ideas, and emotions that they are winning each important personal victory now. Winners practice constantly, on and off the field, in and out of school, in whatever career they choose.

Against the Odds

Need some inspiration? History is full of people who have made it on their own through strong determination against all the odds. Helen Keller (1888–1968) was blind and deaf since infancy, yet with the help of a dedicated teacher she learned to speak and read. A determined teacher in France, Louis Braille (1809–1852), blind since age three, invented a system in 1829 to help sightless people read. Many people still use the Braille system today.

Jim Abbott, professional baseball pitcher, was born without a right hand. Although kids teased him, he went on to excel in both baseball and football in high school and then went on to play in the Majors.

Self-discipline is action! When Winners are in crisis, they work and practice to toughen themselves. They know that imagination is the greatest tool in the universe. It *is* the universe to a prisoner of war.

Winners never quit. Winners never give up. Winners pick themselves up, dust themselves off, and do it all over again . . . better! Discipline yourself to win. Practice "within" when you are "without."

Self-Talk

Again and again, it is the concept of self-talk that helps us discipline ourselves and shape our thinking and actions. Through self-talk, we prepare what we will say before a group, go over how we will perform on the playing field, practice what we want to communicate to the boss. When we do well, we can tell ourselves, "That's more like me." When we perform below what we feel we are capable of, we can tell ourselves, "Next time I'll do better" and then replay the situation in our imagination the way we want it to take place.

Winners use self-talk to coach themselves to do better.

Discipline focuses on self-control. The meaning of self-control is often misunderstood. Some will say it is "getting a good grip on yourself" or staying calm under pressure. Good **self-control** is really

self-determination: taking responsibility for determining the path your life travels. Life is a do-it-yourself workshop in which you construct your own destiny.

You Make It Happen

Some people believe that fate, luck, an astrological sign, or some other force outside their control shapes the outcome of their lives. People who feel that life is determined by chance circumstances or by being in the right place at the right time are more likely to doubt and fear their future than people who know they are in control. People who feel that they do not control what happens to them believe they are victims of circumstance. They simply float along wherever the current of life takes them. These people have not taken responsibility for their successes or failures.

Winners accept the responsibility for taking control of their lives.

Some people have trouble making up their minds because they fear making the wrong choices. They may know they have the potential to control their own lives but do not take a firm stand, do not risk breaking out of the mold to aim higher. They have not persuaded themselves that they should be in control of their choices and decisions. People who think this way have difficulty setting their goals, reaching their goals, and fulfilling their ambitions.

Only when you realize that you are the master of your own destiny can you set a life plan and follow it. Self-control is a powerful tool, and we must use it to the fullest advantage if we are to achieve the things we want, if we are to achieve success.

Play Your Hand

We are given a set of characteristics at birth, but we make the decisions that determine whether we win or lose the game of life. We have to ask ourselves who we are and how we got where we are. The 18th-century French writer Voltaire compared life to a game of cards. Each player is dealt a certain hand. This hand is the personality, characteristics, and family environment that are given to us. We as players must take control and determine how to play that hand, what to keep and what to toss out. We decide how to shape our lives.

No matter who you are, you are responsible for where you are right now and where you go from here. Responsibility means taking control. Ask yourself, "Am I steering my own ship, or am I a victim of the winds of fate?" Are you doing things in life because you want to do them or because you feel they have been forced upon you? People who allow themselves to be pressured into doing things they would rather not do have given up control of their lives to other people. Winning is taking responsibility for your life.

The key to positive self-control is letting go of past failures and disappointments and taking responsibility for your present and future actions. Don't leave your potential to chance. Don't stand back and let things happen to you—make them happen!

Winners choose their actions to take control of their futures.

Just about everything in life is a choice. You don't have to work, go to school, eat, or even get up in the morning. You decide to do things because they are good for you. Often, we are victims of habit: We do things only because we have been doing them. As children, we look to adults to give us cues for behavior. When we mature and become adults, we must make decisions and be responsible for ourselves.

Visualize your desired goals when you are relaxed. This may be early in the morning when you wake up, during a walk, commuting to work or school, or before you go to sleep at night. Never give up rehearsing your goals. Winning is a learned habit. It takes days and weeks of constant practice to overcome old attitudes and lifestyles. It does not happen overnight. Make winning your habit.

Let's take a closer look at some of the points Dr. Waitley discussed and learn how to use the principle of self-discipline in our everyday lives.

The Importance of Self-Discipline

The word *discipline* comes from the Latin word meaning "to teach." Self-discipline is really about teaching ourselves. We are the students and the teachers at the same time. When we have strong self-discipline, we teach ourselves to act in appropriate and positive ways. We learn to act in these ways even when we are tired or restless or bored.

Self-discipline can take many forms. You need to use self-discipline to stick to your study schedule when you want to go to the movies. You need discipline to push yourself away from the table instead of eating dessert. You need to discipline yourself to get assignments handed in by their deadlines. Self-discipline is staying on track in order to reach your goals, no matter how impossible they seem or how hopeless you feel. Self-discipline is the method by which we keep our actions true to our dreams.

James Michener, successful author, once said, "Character consists of what you do on the third and fourth tries." In other words, keep working toward your goal even if you didn't have success on the first or second try. Don't give up! Country singer Randy Travis didn't give up even after being turned down more than once by every recording studio in Nashville. He kept trying for 10 years before becoming an "overnight success." He says, "I'm kind of one to believe that if you work hard at something long enough and keep believing, sooner or later it will happen."

Practice self-discipline to work toward your goals.

Self-discipline means keeping your behavior on track even when your attitude slips a little. You and you alone are responsible for your behavior.

Making Choices

Psychologists tell us that our choices and actions affect how we feel about ourselves. Most of us would agree that you don't have to feel bad about yourself just because you made some poor choices. Taking responsibility for your choices is a basic part of building self-discipline. A willingness to see things the way they are, not just the way we wish they were, is another important element of self-discipline.

Sometimes we feel out of control, as though we have no ability to change the situation. Actually, it is surprising to realize how much we really are in control of things. Sometimes we are in control only of little things, but they add up. When you can exercise control over the little events in your life, you will find that you are taking care of the bigger events as well.

Control big problems with a series of small steps.

For instance, suppose your instructor says you are at risk of failing the geography course you need to get your Travel and Tourism diploma. This, of course, is a big problem. Big problems, though, do not usually spring up overnight. Perhaps your grade is low because you haven't studied enough. By exercising self-discipline, you can stick to your study schedule more closely. When you study well, you will have more time for fun. By using self-discipline for small problems ("Should I read that chapter or go to the movies instead?"), you will avoid a big problem (failing geography).

Self-discipline means deciding to make the most of each moment, not waste it. Consider these situations:

Choose to make the best use of your time.

- *Time spent at school.* You can choose to let your mind wander, or you can decide that you want to become an expert in this subject. You can dream up dozens of questions to ask the instructor and plan how you will tackle the next assignment. With some self-discipline, you can teach yourself to have this attitude toward all your classes.
- *Time spent waiting.* In between classes, on the bus, in line, in a traffic jam—you have complete control over how you react to these situations. You could get angry or frustrated and choose to waste a few minutes, or you could just as easily choose to check your homework on the bus, jot down a list of things to do while you are standing in line, or simply enjoy looking at interesting houses along the street while you are stuck in a traffic jam. With self-discipline, you can choose to make all your free moments productive ones.
- *Communication.* When someone is talking to you and you are starting to tune out, you can decide instead to start listening harder. What is that person trying to say? Can you provide some answers or some feedback? You can decide to be a terrific listener.
- *Daydreams.* It is a lot of fun to daydream. When you set aside a few minutes at the end of the day to relax, you can discipline

yourself to daydream about some new goals. You can picture yourself passing an exam or getting a job interview. Envision yourself five years in the future as a success in the career you are studying.

Self-discipline means being true to yourself and honest about your goals. It is understanding what you want out of life and how to get it, and knowing you are going to work for it and not letting anything stop you—not even yourself.

⌐ *Breaking Bad Habits*

We also can control the habits we have. Dr. Waitley talked about bad habits and how important it is to replace them with good ones. Many of us have to make several attempts at breaking a bad habit before we succeed. Suppose you try 10 times to break a bad habit, and not until the tenth attempt do you succeed. Does that mean you failed nine times? Does it mean you had no self-discipline? No, it means that with each attempt your goal got closer and your self-discipline got stronger, until you beat the habit. As American humorist Mark Twain once said, "Habit is habit, and not to be flung out of the window, but coaxed downstairs a step at a time."

Each time you try, you are one step closer to achieving your goal. Keep going!

Bad habits are not always easy to break. Your bad habits may be quite stubborn, but you can be more so. The more you take control of your life, the easier it will be to break bad habits and form good ones.

Using positive self-talk can be an effective way to break a bad habit. Self-talk can help you solve a problem by changing your actions. Many familiar bad habits—procrastinating, smoking, overeating, oversleeping, and being late—can all be helped with positive self-talk.

Habit-changing self-talk refuses to accept the old habit. It can help you paint a new picture of yourself acting and behaving in a positive way, creating a new habit pattern to replace the old one. An important part of self-talk is persuading your subconscious mind that the change has already taken place. Instead of saying, "I will stop being late," you can say, "I arrive on time." The idea is that by thinking of yourself as someone who is on time, you will start to be on time. If you say that you will start being on time in the future, you are implying that right now you are still being late. As long as you see yourself in the present moment as having a bad habit, you will continue to act as if you do.

State your goal as fact and it will be easier to achieve.

Self-talk can begin with single sentences:

- I arrive on time for all my classes.
- I am proud of myself when I arrive on time.
- Being on time shows respect for the instructor and for the rest of the class.
- Arriving on time shows that I am a responsible person.

The more you use positive self-talk, the more your new self-image and new behavior will become part of your personality. By that time, you will have really kicked the bad habit and replaced it with something more positive. What an accomplishment! What could be better for your self-esteem!

Taking Responsibility

Self-discipline also means taking responsibility for your life and everything in it. It means knowing you are in control, knowing you have the power to change things, and feeling good about it. Psychologists call this feeling **empowerment**. You can empower yourself by taking control of your life.

Empower yourself (give yourself the power) to succeed by taking control of your life.

We can develop the power to change things that make us unhappy. It is important to realize, however, that we cannot control other people. If someone close to us is having problems, sometimes we have to separate ourselves from those problems. We may have control over our lives, but the people in our lives have control over themselves. Likewise, we don't let other people control who and what we are.

General Colin Powell was the Chairman of the Joint Chiefs of Staff during the Persian Gulf War. He grew up in the South Bronx, one of the poorest, most crime-filled neighborhoods in America. One day he went back to that neighborhood to give a speech to students at his old high school. He told the students: "If you are black, if you're Puerto Rican or Hispanic, be proud of that. But don't let it become a problem. Let it become somebody else's problem." Powell didn't want students to see themselves as "victims," powerless to change their lives. He wanted them to understand that they too could become "empowered" and work toward their dreams without blaming others for their start in life or for any of the hardships along the way.

Getting Support

Exercising our self-discipline can help us if we find ourselves having trouble maintaining our schedules. Sometimes we may find ourselves feeling overwhelmed, feeling that we have taken on too much. Using our self-discipline to set priorities and manage our time can help relieve those feelings of stress.

The key is to recognize the problem and get help. We can ask family members or friends, or take turns being helped by or helping someone else who needs it. Most schools have a support staff that can point students in the right direction. The staff can help with tutoring and other kinds of study assistance. Advisers and instructors also may be able to provide helpful advice.

Choosing Positive Attitudes

There is a natural law of cause and effect. This means that for every action we take, there will be a reaction. Our lives and our successes will reflect how we use our minds, skills, and talents. This again is about accepting responsibility, making choices, taking control.

Choose positive actions to achieve positive effects.

Building up self-discipline begins with taking a good look at yourself and your attitudes, both positive and negative. It is up to you to decide what is positive, helpful, and worth keeping, and what is negative, harmful, and holding you back. Your attitudes are a powerful part of your personality and can either help or hurt your chances for success. Choose a winning attitude today!

S C E N E

5–2

R I C K ' S   S T O R Y

Rick learns to organize his time.

Rick wanted to earn his certificate, but he felt overwhelmed by all the work he needed to do to be successful. He figured he could get by studying on the bus and during breaks at work. When he failed Tuesday's English exam because he hadn't studied enough, he knew he needed to better organize his time. Rick spoke with his adviser.

"I know you have a lot of work, Rick, but it's nothing you can't handle," his adviser said. "You just need to be more disciplined. You need to set aside time to study every day, and not just leave things to chance."

"OK," Rick agreed. "But what about having some fun? I want to spend some time with my kids, and I can't do that if I spend all my time studying and working and going to classes."

"Once you start to discipline yourself and manage your time better, you will get more work done," Rick's adviser told him. "You will find there is more free time in that busy schedule than you thought."

Rick decided to take this advice. The first thing he did was buy an appointment calendar. He wrote down all his assignments and appointments, and planned some study time into every day. Rick found that writing things down on paper helped him set priorities and get the really important jobs done first. He had a new sense of empowerment over his day. He also found that now he had the information he needed to make better choices concerning the use of his time.

It wasn't always easy, but Rick was determined to succeed. His favorite self-talk statement was "I choose to make the time to study so that I do well in my classes." That choice of words reminded him that he was in control and it was his choice to study. It also reinforced the fact that he would be able to do well in his classes. When he was standing in line at the grocery store, he found himself visualizing himself in business attire, sitting at a desk in front of his computer, planning an around-the-world trip for an important client. It made him feel good to think of the trust that the client would have in his ability to take care of all the details for such a large trip. Even though this was just a daydream, he began to feel competent and successful.

One night, some of Rick's friends invited him to go see a movie with them, but he didn't go because he had a test the next day to study for. He was glad he had made the choice to study, because he earned a B+ and felt really good about his effort. He began to see how his self-discipline was starting to pay off.

THOUGHT-PROVOKING   QUESTIONS

1.   Dr. Waitley mentioned "doing within" while "doing without."
How can self-discipline help someone who has little money or
emotional support?

2.   Why will the self-talk statement "I arrive on time" be more
effective than the statement "I will stop being late"? Why is the
second sentence considered negative? How can visualization
help to break bad habits?

3.   When a horoscope comes true, is it because fate is controlling
your future, or is it because you have subconsciously accepted
the prediction as your goal? Can you empower yourself to control your future?

4.   In the Chinese language, the symbol for "crisis" is the combination of symbols meaning "danger" and "opportunity." Do you
think these words make sense together? Why or why not? Write
about a crisis (or opportunity) in your life right now that would
benefit from your self-discipline and control.

5.   Does the advice to take control of your life contradict the advice
to develop a good support system?

Time-Demand Survey

Have you noticed that the "self" qualities you studied in Chapters 2–4 (self-awareness, self-image, and self-esteem) are united within the person named You? Self-discipline, or your ability to develop habits in line with your goals, interacts with the other aspects of "self." For example, positive self-talk alone will not raise your self-esteem.

Have you heard the phrase "walk the talk"? It means that what you do is in line with what you say. The expression applies to self-talk. Words have power, but they have more power when backed up by day-to-day habits that keep your self-talk in sync with how you act or live.

Many of your everyday actions depend on how you use time. Becoming self-disciplined involves "getting a handle" on how you use your time, instead of letting time use you. Activity 5–1 is designed to help you with this important step.

Instructions:

1. *How much time in hours (rounded to the nearest quarter hour) do you now spend per week in each of these areas? Enter your response on the line.*
   Example: g. Personal hygiene/grooming.   8¾

Areas   *Hours*

a. Class attendance.   _____

b. Commuting (to and from school or work).   _____

c. Eating meals and snacks.   _____

d. Family responsibilities (childcare, housekeeping, shopping, etc.).   _____

e. Job and career planning/preparation.   _____

f. Leisure activities pursued alone (hobbies, television, etc.).   _____

g. Personal hygiene/grooming.   _____

h. Physical exercise.   _____

i. Religious activities.   _____

j. Sleeping.   _____

k. Social (building/maintaining friendships; group activities/events.)   _____

   Subtotal   (a–k)   _____

l.   List the number of credits you are taking.   _____

m.   Multiply this number (k) by 2 (representing two hours of study time per credit).   _____

Subtotal   (l + m)   _____

Total   (add subtotals)   _____

_____

Scoring

If your total for this survey is greater than 168, you are overcommitted. A week contains 168 hours. Needless to say, if the claims on your time exceed the time available, you need to ask yourself, what is a time demand? Is several hours of television every evening a demand on your time, or is it a choice? Does your school demand that you attend every football and basketball game, or can you miss a game sometimes to do things you value even more?

If your total for the survey is less than 160 hours, you let time "get away from you." You let the equivalent of a night's sleep or day's work slip out of your control. Where do those hours go? In which area(s) would you choose to spend those "missing" hours?

2.   *Go over your numbers in the time-demand survey. List below the areas to which you give less than two hours a week.*

_____

_____

_____

_____

_____

_____

3.   *In this list (Step 2), check (✓) those areas on which you want to spend more time. On the lines below, write each of the checked areas. Then, in parentheses, list specific things in those areas that you would do if you could "find the time." Example: Religious activities (attend a service, take a class, listen to inspirational tapes).*

_____   (_____)

_____   (_____)

_____   (_____)

_____   (_____)

4. Go back again to the areas in Step 1. If you are overcommitted (total greater than 168 hours), do you spend more time in any area than you need and want to? If so, list the area(s). If you "lose" time (total less than 161 hours), try to list the ways in which your time is "lost."

_____

_____

_____

_____

_____

_____

Using Self-Discipline

In Activity 5–1, you focused on ways in which you use the 10,080 minutes, or 168 hours, in a typical week. Perhaps you are not entirely pleased with what the Time-Demand Survey showed you and would like to change some of your time-use habits. As you just read, you can, through the process of self-discipline, teach yourself new habits to replace old ones. First, as Dr. Waitley stated, you have to want to change.

In this activity, you will think of ways you can apply self-discipline to using time more effectively. Remember, self-discipline is part of more self-awareness, a better self-image, and higher self-esteem. Self-discipline is a tool for shaping yourself into the person you want to (can) be.

Instructions:

1. *In the spaces provided, list at least three ways you can use more self-discipline in each area. Focus on information you listed in Activity 5–1, Step 3. List only changes that you can make. (Some changes may be desirable but not in your control right now. Omit such changes from your list.) Keep in mind that even though many areas are listed here, you are only one person. Although you are listing many changes in many areas, you are not expected to make all these changes at once. Consider all your responsibilities when thinking of your planned changes. Remember that small, achievable changes are better than large ones that never happen; progress often comes in small steps.*
   Use a separate sheet of paper if you need extra space.

   Example: School: class attendance, commuting, and study/homework
   a. *Attend all class meetings unless a real emergency arises.*
   b. *Leave for class 15 minutes earlier to plan for possible traffic jams.*
   c. *Set aside one extra hour a week to practice keyboarding skills.*

Area: includes, but is not limited to, these related activities

Community: volunteer work, religious participation, neighborhood events

a. _____

b. _____

c. _____

Family: housekeeping, shopping, meal planning and preparation, money management

a. _____

b. _____

c. _____

Job: commuting, gaining new knowledge or skills, relating to supervisor and co-workers

a. _____

b. _____

c. _____

Leisure/social: hobbies, television, sporting events, concerts, and so on

a. _____

b. _____

c. _____

Personal fitness: exercise, hygiene/grooming, eating and sleeping habits

a. _____

b. _____

c. _____

School: class attendance, commuting, and study/homework

a. _____

b. _____

c. _____

2. *Review the lists of possible changes (Step 1). Select any three that you believe would make the biggest difference in your life. Copy them below.*

a. _____

b. _____

c. _____

3. *What will you do today to initiate these important changes (Step 2)?*

    _____

    _____

    _____

4. *When will you return to this page to repeat Steps 2 and 3 on the changes you did not select this time? Dates:*

    _____ , _____ , _____ ,

5. *Write a summary of what you learned from the Time-Demand Survey about your time usage. What, if any, actions will you take to change it?*

    _____

    _____

    _____

6. *Turn to p. 243 (the first page of Chapter 9) and write a note in the margin: Redo the Time-Demand Survey on p. 129 (this page).*

Overcoming Obstacles

Self-discipline and positive self-talk must go hand in hand. You may be familiar with the expression "talk is cheap," which means that talk unsupported by action is not enough. Be sure that the positive self-talk you practice (see Activity 4–4) is reinforced by steady positive action (self-discipline). Here are some hints to help you.

* Decide you want to change your self-thoughts and actions.
* Zero in on just what thoughts or habits you want to alter.
* Choose replacements for old ways of thinking and acting. (Remember, no one actually breaks, or wipes out, an old habit or thought pattern. Instead, you replace the old with the new.)
* Start changing. The word *start* here means that change doesn't happen when you decide to do it or when you begin "looking on the bright side." Lasting change takes time, and it takes work. New habits have to be repeated many, many times to erase lifelong habits. That's where self-discipline comes in.

Listed below are some obstacles, or barriers, that people often say prevent them from getting what they want out of life. Perhaps some of these things have been obstacles for you.

Instructions:

1. *In this list, put a check mark in the blank next to those items that are problems in your life.*

_____ Not enough education.		_____ Overweight.
_____ Not enough money.		_____ Too short.
_____ Bad economy.		_____ Too tall.
_____ Uncooperative husband/wife.		_____ Can't establish credit.
_____ In-laws don't like me.		_____ Never get the right job.
_____ Ethnic background.		_____ Inflation.
_____ Live in a bad neighborhood.		_____ Boss doesn't realize my talents.
_____ Parents don't treat me fairly.		_____ The government.
_____ Friends have a bad influence.		_____ Too many people depend on me.
_____ Instructors don't like me.		

2. *Can you name other obstacles in your life that are not on the list? Add them below.*

_____   _____

_____   _____

_____   _____

_____   _____

3. *Consider the items you have checked. Items that you cannot control (too short, ethnic background, the government) are obstacles that can be overcome mainly with self-talk. Items that you can control (overweight, perhaps) need not only talk but action on your part. In these cases, your self-talk acts as fuel to keep self-discipline on track. Beside each check mark in Steps 1 and 2, write C if you can control the obstacle; write N if you cannot control it.*

4. *List an obstacle you checked on the top line in each set of lines below. List the C (controllable) barriers first, followed by the N (not controllable) ones. You will complete the Talk & Action portions in Step 5.*

Obstacle: _____

Talk & Action: _____

_____

Obstacle: _____

Talk & Action: _____

_____

Obstacle: _____

Talk & Action: _____

_____

Obstacle: _____

Talk & Action: _____

_____

Obstacle: _____

Talk & Action: _____

_____

5. *Use the ideas of self-talk and self-discipline to suggest a way to overcome each obstacle (Step 4). In the following example, note that responsible action (applied for a student loan) backs up the positive talk (I know I'll have enough money . . .).*

   Obstacle: Not enough money

   Talk & Action: Now that I've applied for a student loan, I know I'll have enough money for the rest of the quarter.

6. *Did you check any obstacles in Step 1 that you did not turn into a positive Talk & Action statement? If so, write that obstacle in the following space. Then write a paragraph explaining how that obstacle differs from the others in this activity.*

   _____

   _____

   _____

   _____

   _____

   _____

   _____

   _____

   _____

Attendance Chart

Success involves self-discipline. Success at school means regular class attendance—showing up on time every class, prepared to receive from and contribute to the instructor and other students in the class. If school attendance is a problem area, Activity 5–4 is designed for you. The activity is for you even if school attendance isn't a problem in your life. The attendance chart is an example of self-discipline that you can apply to other areas.

Instructions:

1. *On the chart below, list each of your classes in the left-hand column.*

2. *For a week, keep track of your attendance.*

    a. *Record a symbol in the square for each day of the week, as follows.*
       - *Arrive on time and "ready":* ✳
       - *Arrive on time, not fully prepared:* ✓
       - *Arrive a few minutes late:* −
       - *Miss a class:* ☹

    b. *At the end of the class period, write a comment in the right-hand column. The remark should tell how you feel about the class. (Remember to do Steps a and b for every class, every day, for a whole week.)*

    c. *At the end of the week, write a summary of your class attendance and the outcomes of it. Answer these questions in your summary:*
       - *How well did you do in each class?*
       - *Do you see a connection between attendance and performance?*
       - *What are the benefits of attending class regularly?*
       - *Did your class attendance leave room for improvement? If so, what can you do to improve it?*
       - *Did you reinforce your self-discipline (attending class) by writing positive self-talk in the Comments column?*

CLASS ATTENDANCE (SELF-DISCIPLINE) CHART						
Class	M	T	W	Th	F	Comments
Summary:						

3. *Could a similar chart help you solve other problems? List two or three other problems for which a similar chart might work. Choose one of the problems and use the following space to create a self-discipline chart.*

4. *Repeat Steps 1 and 2 of the activity, using your new chart.*

To-Do Chart

As noted in Activity 5–1, Time-Demand Survey, self-discipline is closely related to how you use your time. In that activity, you looked at your time usage habits through a "wide-angle lens." This activity, which involves another chart, gives you a "close-up."

Time management is a common term and a popular idea these days, especially in business. Time is one area in which everyone is created equal. No one has more time or less time than you. Every one of us has exactly 10,080 minutes a week. We do differ in how we use those minutes. Winners decide what's important to them in the long term. Then they plan carefully to spend most of their time doing those important things.

What are the advantages of using a to-do chart? Several are listed below. You will likely be able to add to the list once you've used such a chart.

- Writing down the tasks you must do keeps you from worrying about forgetting a task.
- Keeping a chart helps you separate things that matter from busywork. ("Staying busy" is not what to-do charts are about. The point is to use time on things that have long-term importance to you and the significant people in your life.)
- Charting helps you complete tasks on schedule. By deciding when a task must be started in order to be done on time, you can break the lateness habit.
- Checking off a finished task prompts you to start the next one. The check marks give you a visual reminder that you are a productive person.
- By scheduling a week in advance, you can build in leisure time and still complete the to-do items. Weekly planning lets you pace yourself.
- Planning for a week, instead of a day, helps you avoid wasted time starting and stopping. Each time you put down a task and take up a different one, time is lost before you "get into" the new task.
- A chart prevents setting yourself up for failure by trying to do more than can be done in a week. Remember, a chart doesn't add hours, and everyone has the same number of hours each week.

Instructions:

1. List all the tasks you must do in the next week on the lines below. Omit the obvious things, such as eating meals, sleeping, and bathing. Do include basic maintenance tasks, such as grocery shopping.

_____   _____   _____

_____   _____   _____

_____   _____   _____

_____   _____   _____

_____   _____   _____

_____   _____   _____

2. Review the list. Cross out any tasks that are neither required of you nor important to you.

3. Enter the remaining activities (Step 1) in the left-hand column of the following to-do chart.

To-Do Chart			
Task	Due Date	Importance	Day and Time

4. In the Due Date column, write the date by which the task must be done.

5. *In the Importance column, assign a number to each task listed.*

       Very important: 1
       Important: 2
       Somewhat important: 3

6. *In the right-hand column, set a day to do each number 1 task, starting with the number 1 tasks with the earliest due date. (Keep a list of your appointments in front of you so that you won't plan to complete a task when you're already set to do something else.) Repeat this step for number 2 tasks, then number 3 tasks.*

7. *Refer to the to-do chart throughout each day and make every effort to stick to it. (Your accuracy will improve as you continue using the chart.) As you complete each task, put a large ✓ over it.*

8. *If the chart doesn't seem to be working after two or three days, instead of giving up, create a new chart on a separate sheet by repeating Steps 1–7. Keep at it; you can make it work for you.*

9. *Decide when you will do your to-do chart for the next week. Friday afternoon? Sunday night? Monday morning? Write your choice here:* _____

10. *At the end of two weeks (put a reminder on your calendar now), write a letter to a younger student who has asked you to name some benefits of using a to-do chart.*

                                                                               _____
(Today's date)

Dear _____

_____

_____

_____

_____

_____

_____

_____

_____

                                        Cordially

                                        _____
(Your Name)

One must not lose desires. They are mighty stimulants to creativeness, to love, and to long life.

Alexander Bogomoletz

6

Psychology of Self-Motivation

CHAPTER OBJECTIVES

After you read this chapter and complete the activities, you will:

- See how fear, desire, and other emotions can affect motivation.

- Be able to determine if your goals are good ones.

- Be able to find the motivation in yourself to go after your goals.

- Be able to use positive self-talk and visualization to motivate yourself.

- Be able to take risks and make opportunities for yourself.

S C E N E
6–1

☙

D I A N E ' S   S T O R Y

"What difference does it make?"

No matter what Diane was supposed to do or where Diane was supposed to be, she would be late. Her friends had learned to adjust their schedules to make allowances for Diane's lateness.

Diane just didn't see the need to be on time and believed that her time was too valuable to ever arrive somewhere early. She thought that she was being very efficient because by arriving a few minutes late, she was avoiding the crowd.

No one ever challenged Diane until she went back to school to get her GED. One day her instructor told her that if she couldn't start coming to class on time, she shouldn't come at all.

"Actually," said the instructor, "I think it would be a good idea for you to speak with an adviser about this problem."

Diane disagreed. "What's the big deal?" she asked herself. "I'm 37 years old and have done OK up until now. I don't have to show up on time to get a good grade—I'm passing. I'm not keeping anybody else from showing up on time."

"If I miss some of the discussion, I can just get the notes from somebody else in the class. I don't see what the big deal is."

"I am tired of all the hassle for being late. It doesn't seem like they
do anything important before I get here anyway."

Can you think of any reasons that would make Diane
want to be on time?

A   T A L K   W I T H   D R .   W A I T L E Y

Dr. Waitley discusses self-motivation and the drive within us. He tells us that self-motivation can help us overcome fear and help us see risk as opportunity.

What Is Self-Motivation?

Everything we do is the result of motivation. It may be positive or negative, intentional or unintentional, a little or a lot. Motivation can be learned or developed—we don't have to be born with it. Motivation is a force that moves us to action, and it springs from inside us.

It has often been thought that motivation, like gasoline to a car, can be pumped in from the outside through pep talks, rallies, or sermons. These can provide encouragement or inspiration for a person to act, but the person has to have the **desire**. Lasting change can happen only when the individual understands and feels the need inside. The person must want the reward in order to become motivated.

Winners desire to achieve their goals.

Motivation moves you in the direction of goals you have set. Even in the face of mistakes, discouragement, and setbacks, your positive inner drive keeps you moving ahead. Motivation is an emotional state. The great physical and mental motivations are survival, hunger, thirst, revenge, and love. Two strong emotions that are opposites of one another are part of motivation: fear and desire.

Fear is one of the most powerful emotions that can affect motivation in a negative way. Fear makes you panic, often needlessly, and it can defeat goals. The opposite emotion, desire, is like a strong positive magnet. It attracts and encourages plans and goals. Fear and desire are far apart and lead to opposite destinies. Fear looks to the past. Desire looks to the future. Fear remembers past pain, disappointment, failure, and unpleasantness and reminds us that these experiences can be repeated. Desire triggers memories of pleasure and success and excites the need to create new winning experiences.

A Winner's motivation is positive and looks to the future.

The fearful person says, "I have to," "I can't," "I see risk," and "I wish." The person with desire says, "I want to," "I can," "I see opportunity," and "I will." Desire is the emotional state between where you are and where you want to be. Winners have desire. They are not content with the way things are now. They want change for the better.

Positive Tension

Positive tension is an inner drive produced by motivation. It is like a bow pulled back tight to shoot an arrow to the bull's-eye on a target. Winners respond to stress in a healthy way. It helps them reach for goals that are worthy of them.

Winners respond to stress with a positive tension.

Actors often get nervous "butterflies" in their stomachs before a performance. This is natural and positive and often gets the adrenaline pumping for a good show. Pro football player Jerry Rice says, "Butterflies tell me the fire is still inside." Butterflies are nice. When they start to eat at you, however, they are like moths. Moths in your stomach are not nice and can even cause ulcers.

Since we always move in the direction of what we are thinking of most, it is important to concentrate our thoughts on what we want to achieve rather than try to move away from what we fear.

The mind cannot concentrate on the opposite of an idea. Instead of saying, "I shouldn't use the car to travel short distances," we can tell ourselves, "I will walk and ride my bike more." Focus on what you will do, not on what you won't do. Concentrate on one good thought at a time, on the winning action.

Winners focus on what they will do.

Take the game of basketball, for example. Imagine your only job is to concentrate on one foul shot. You discipline yourself to think only of that shot and eliminate everything else from your mind. There is no room for negatives, only the one positive task at hand. Visualize the outcome you want. Picture yourself making the perfect shot. Shoot for the stars! What you think about is likely to be what you achieve.

The only limits to what we can achieve are limits we put on ourselves. Laziness is one roadblock. ("Why should I bother?") Fear is another. ("It's too risky for me".)

It isn't just fear of failure that holds us back. It is often fear of success. If we can't see our potential and what we can do, we are beaten from the start. We make the excuse, "It is not worth it to succeed." What we are really saying is, "I am not worth the effort." Low self-esteem and poor self-image are major reasons that we fail to reach our goals.

Risk As Opportunity

Winners see risk as opportunity. They see the rewards of success before it happens. They do not fear failure, and they accept the risk or the opportunity. As Tim McMahon says, "Yes, risk-taking is inherently failure prone. Otherwise it would be called sure-thing-taking." Desire is the answer to fear and despair. Desire sparks activity that positively channels extra adrenaline, which keeps the mind busy, which keeps the hope of achievement alive.

Winners look for opportunities to succeed.

A famous actor once suffered a nervous breakdown before he went on stage. He was ordered to rest and repair his damaged nervous system. He was afraid and had lost all confidence in himself. After awhile, his doctor suggested that he perform before a small group in his town. When the actor said he was terrified of failing, the doctor answered that he was using fear as an excuse, and fear was not a good reason to quit. He told the actor that Winners admit fear and go on in spite of it.

The actor put his fear aside and went on to perform in front of the little group. His performance was a great success, and afterward he realized that he had admitted his fear but hadn't let it stop him. After that night, he pushed himself to perform in front of larger audiences all over the world, knowing that he could overcome the fear and not let it end his acting career. He knew the fear of the unknown might always be there, but that being frightened would never again make him give up.

Winners seek a personal pleasure that comes with achievement.

Some people confuse material gain—making a lot of money or gaining a great deal of power—with achieving success. Do not confuse material success with personal achievement and individual excellence. There is a personal pleasure that comes from achieving the difficult. Healthy self-esteem, pride, and the thrill of reaching a goal are all reasons enough for pursuing your success.

The Winner's Edge

We know that high achievers have high motivation. The power to move them to action comes from inside themselves. There seems to be only a fine line between the top 5 percent of real achievers and Winners and the rest of the pack. You might call this fine line The Winner's Edge.

Self-motivation creates The Winner's Edge.

Think about the difference between simple boiling water and powerful steam. When water is heated to 211 degrees Fahrenheit, it is simply boiling water. Yet when the temperature reaches 212 degrees, only one degree higher, the water becomes steam that is powerful enough to launch a Navy jet from an aircraft carrier to a speed of 120 miles an hour in only five seconds.

ᴄ Modern-Day Heroes

We all know famous people who have achieved great things, but we don't often think of the tough road that led them to their goals. Olympic gold-medal sprinter Gail Devers was diagnosed with a serious illness and at one point almost had to have her feet amputated. Gail didn't let her misfortunes stop her; she battled her illness and went on to become the world's fastest woman at the Barcelona games. Major-league pitcher Dave Dravecky made a spectacular comeback after fighting cancer. Actress and talk-show host Oprah Winfrey grew up poor in a small town in Mississippi. She worked hard to achieve her dreams, letting nothing discourage her or get in her way. Today she is one of the richest and most powerful women in the entertainment industry.

Winners share a desire to win, teamed with drive, focus, and persistence.

These individuals all wanted something special for themselves and wouldn't allow themselves to be held back by bad luck or unhappy circumstances. They all had the desire to win, and they expected to win. Success is not only for the privileged; you don't have to be born rich or talented or strong. Success depends on drive, focus, and persistence. The secret of success is to make the extra effort, try another approach, concentrate on the desired outcome. Out of desire comes the energy and will to win. Get that urge to win!

Let's take a closer look at some of the points Dr. Waitley discussed and learn how to use the principle of self-motivation in our everyday lives.

✍ The Importance of Self-Motivation

Motivation is the force within us that drives us to do something. We may be motivated to do something or not. We may be driven toward a situation or away from it, depending on how we feel inside. When we have important goals to achieve, motivating ourselves is one of the first steps in achieving them.

✍ Some Views on Motivation

Erich Fromm, a leading figure in psychiatry and psychoanalysis, was concerned with people's drives rather than their behavior. He said people should judge themselves by their "passions," or their desire to experience life in an intense and useful way.

Another famous psychologist, B.F. Skinner, believed that experience determines behavior. He said that environment and surroundings play an important role in motivating people to behave in a certain way. He suggested that people do what they do because of what happens when they do it. If people do something and find some sort of "reward," or something good happens, they will likely continue to do it. If people do something and find "punishment," or something bad happens, they likely will not do it again.

Motivation depends on pleasure and rewards.

Psychologist Abraham Maslow knew that we are motivated by our subconscious minds and by the environment, yet he also believed that we can control our behavior. He believed that we are motivated for two important reasons:

1.   Because an activity is pleasurable, and doing it will give us satisfaction.
2.   Because we will get some additional reward outside the activity.

For example, you might be studying math because you really enjoy it. Or you might be taking the course because it is required to achieve your goal of graduation.

Human beings are motivated by needs and wants. We need things like food, clothing, and shelter to survive; we want things like a loving relationship, a comfortable home, and a job we like.

☞ *Values and Motivation*

Dr. Waitley often mentions the importance of being able to focus on what we want to achieve. Author Paul R. Timm, in his book *Successful Self-Management*, points out that values can give us that focus in our lives. When our values are unclear, finding a direction can be difficult, and we may have trouble deciding what our true goals are for the future.

Your values will affect your goals and motivations.

Your values have a direct effect on what motivates you. Values are beliefs that you hold to be important: succeeding in your job, taking care of your children, obeying the law, having friends, being healthy, having money. Timm suggests that we ask ourselves the following questions:

- What are my greatest abilities?
- What are my greatest liabilities, or negative things about me?
- What are my goals for this year?
- What are my goals for next year?

Motivation is a combination of ideas, needs, wants, feelings, and conditions that cause us to act in a certain way. This combination is constantly changing as we grow and mature. This explains why we often look at things we have done and ask, "Why did I do that? What was I thinking of?" We cannot always remember what motivated us in the past to act a certain way, now that our values and motivations are different.

You determine your own values and motivations.

Everyone has different values. Author Rita Baltus tells the story of a kind missionary who had gone to a poverty-stricken nation to help people in need. Two tourists visiting the country saw the missionary carefully cleaning a man who had leprosy, a terrible skin disease. One tourist turned to the other and said, "I wouldn't do that for a million dollars." The missionary looked up and replied, "Neither would I." Clearly the missionary was motivated by something other than money.

☞ *Examining Your Goals*

Successful people take responsibility for their life situations. Motivation comes from within each of us, and therefore it is our responsibility to motivate ourselves. If you are not getting closer to your goals, don't allow yourself to lose motivation; find out why you are stuck. Remember that motivation will not always stay at the same high level. As you experience setbacks, you must renew your motivation. To do this, you must sometimes review your goals and revise them or set new ones.

Examine your goals to renew your motivation.

Have you set a reasonable time limit in which to achieve your goals? Do you have the kind of support system you need? Perhaps the goal itself needs to be changed in some way. In her book *Career Directions*, job-placement expert Donna J. Yena observes that well-set goals have the following characteristics:

- A goal should be conceivable.
  Can you picture the goal in your mind?
- A goal should be believable.
  Do you really believe it can happen?
- A goal should be desirable.
  Do you really want it?
- A goal should be achievable.
  Is it realistic?
- A goal should be measurable.
  Can you set a time frame for evaluating whether or not you have achieved it?

Is the following example—to lose weight—a well-set goal? Let's examine it against Yena's characteristics. Your self-awareness and self-image will determine whether or not the goal is conceivable, believable, and desirable. The goal is conceivable if you can picture it in your mind. Only you will be able to determine if a goal is believable and desirable. This goal is achievable, but is it measurable? How much weight do you desire to lose and in what amount of time?

You might revise the goal to "I want to lose 15 pounds by next Saturday." This goal, although measurable, desirable, and possibly conceivable, is no longer believable or achievable. In other words, you might want it, but it just isn't a realistic goal. More revision is necessary.

Instead try, "I will lose one pound a week for the next 15 weeks by watching my diet and walking for one-half hour every day." You are motivated and have decided to lose some weight, so the goal is conceivable, believable, and desirable. The goal is certainly measurable—15 pounds over a 15-week period with periodic goals of one pound per week. This goal is now achievable because a realistic target has been set. Now that all five elements have been satisfied, we can consider this a well-set goal.

Unless you act immediately, you will lose your motivation.

Remember that for every goal you set, you must take some action immediately before your motivation begins to slip. One of the best ways to take immediate action is to begin your positive self-talk.

Self-Talk

Self-talk can get you motivated. The voice inside that talks to you can motivate you to action. You can tell yourself, "I can do it! I am doing a good job. I keep trying until I get it right." Self-talk helps give you the confidence to work toward your goals and keep on target. You can change what you are by what you put into or allow to go into your mind.

Use self-talk to build your confidence.

Just as positive self-talk can help someone talk herself into a good situation, negative self-talk can help her talk herself out of one. For example, someone might be in the habit of using negative self-talk when she sees an ad in the newspaper for a job she wants. She reads the ad, thinks about it, and says, "They would never hire me for this job," or "For this high a salary they would expect too much from me."

By using positive self-talk, she can encourage herself to take a chance, try to succeed. She might say, "I am well qualified for the job," or "I will let them know how my training and skills make me the best person for the job." If she doesn't try, she will never know if she could have succeeded.

Self-talk can even help you see a situation more clearly. You are more likely to see all sides of an issue when you listen to, question, and think about what you are saying to yourself. Psychoanalyst Paul Horton made a study of the calming effect of self-talk. He conducted a survey of 208 people and found that self-talk ranked among the top 10 ways that people cheered themselves up.

Visualization

After you have examined the situation through self-talk, the next step is visualization. Picture what you want in detail. Picture the final successful result.

Visualize your goal at successful completion.

If your goal is to quit smoking, picture yourself in a situation where you would normally smoke but without a cigarette. See yourself without smoke in the air, breathing easily, and with a smile on your face.

If your goal is to be better organized, picture yourself in your study area with papers neatly filed and supplies in order. See yourself calmly studying or finishing your assignments.

If your goal is to get a part-time job, picture yourself confidently walking into an interview. See yourself as well-groomed, with a professional attitude. Imagine yourself answering the questions without hesitation. Finally, see the employer nodding, smiling, and shaking your hand.

Remind yourself daily of your goal by reading a word picture.

Why does visualization work? Pictures help to excite and inspire us because they involve our emotions. In addition to the picture in your mind, write a word picture with as much detail as possible. Write down what you see in your mind. Read your word picture daily to remind yourself of your goal and to renew your motivation.

The Comfort Zone

Psychologists often speak of the "comfort zone," a place in your mind where you know you feel safe, and you know you can succeed. Most goals, though, require that you move a bit outside your comfort zone in order to reach them. To go after a goal is to move into new areas and to try new things, and doing this can be quite stressful. Since you don't want to become so stressed that you give up your goal, the best course of action is to move outside your comfort zone bit by bit—taking slow, small steps that are challenging but not uncomfortable.

Work toward your goals a little bit every day.

For example, suppose you have decided to go back to school and get your degree in business administration, but you feel overwhelmed by all the different schools, application forms, and tuition fees. Trying to tackle all these things at once would be extremely stressful. You have jumped too far beyond your comfort zone and might even feel like giving up the whole idea. The solution is to approach the project slowly—step by step. You could set aside one afternoon for calling schools and asking for their catalogs. The next day you might set aside an hour to work on a budget to pay for school and set aside a few hours over the weekend to investigate car pools or bus schedules. By breaking up the task into smaller steps, you will feel better able to manage them. You will be on your way to reaching your goal.

The Fear Of Failure

There are many kinds of motivation. You might be surprised to discover that some motivations are negative. For example, fear can be a motivating factor. It can have both positive and negative results.

Jerry Rice believes "fear is good because it brings out the best in people." He believes that when he recognizes failure as a possibility, he achieves more. He says, "Failure scares me and keeps me focused." That focus keeps him from making mistakes. He says, "When you relax, you drop footballs."

Fear can have a negative or positive influence.

If you haven't been studying, and you recently failed several tests, you might be anxious about passing the course; this fear could motivate you to get your study habits back on track. On the negative side, fear, especially the fear of success, can lead to self-defeating behavior—for example, the man who gets so drunk the night before a job interview that he sleeps through his alarm; the student who doesn't study for the final exam; the graduate who keeps "forgetting" to mail in her student-loan payments.

Procrastination

Procrastination is often a symptom of the fear of failure and the fear of success. Many people procrastinate because it gives them an excuse for their failure. They say, "There is no way I could have passed that test; I only had two days to study!"

Some people, on the other hand, are perfectionists: They want so badly to do something perfectly that they consider themselves failures if they do just a "good" job. So they procrastinate and then say they didn't do a great job because there was no time. Perfectionists think success means "perfection," when it really just means doing the best you can to reach your goals. Procrastinating is the surest way to see that your goals remain unfulfilled.

The best step toward your goal is the one you take NOW.

The best way to stop procrastinating is to DO something! Divide your project into small steps and complete just one. Tell yourself you will spend just 15 minutes making an outline for that essay. When you divide a project into smaller segments, you will find it is much less overwhelming. You may even find that you are enjoying your work. The stronger your motivation, the more you will be able to fight the urge to procrastinate. As the popular Nike ad says, "Just Do It."

☞ *Working toward Success*

One well-known baseball player struck out over 1,300 times in his career, an average of one strikeout in every game. At the time he was playing, he had struck out more than anyone else. Perhaps you are thinking this guy wasn't such a great athlete. Actually, that strikeout champion was Hall of Famer Babe Ruth, one of the greatest baseball players in history. Sometimes achieving great victories means working through some defeats along the way.

Concentrate on your successes, not on your failures.

In baseball, a player with a batting average of .300 is considered very skilled indeed. Only the best players can hit that well. A .300 average means that the batter got three hits for every 10 times at bat. Seven times out of 10, the batter failed. However, a .300 batter is a successful one.

Achieving success can be a battle—working your way through one failure after another until you have accomplished your goal. What keeps a person going even after he has been knocked down? Historians like to point out the résumé of one unlucky politician as an example of motivation and determination. Among his few successes, the politician suffered the following failures:

At age
22   Failed in business.
23   Ran for legislature—lost.
24   Failed in business again.
26   Death of sweetheart.
27   Nervous breakdown.
29   Ran for Speaker—lost.
31   Ran for elector—lost.
34   Ran for Congress—lost.
39   Ran for Congress again—lost.
46   Ran for vice president—lost.
49   Ran for Senate—lost.

You might think this unfortunate person had plenty of reason to give up on his dreams, but he didn't. He kept working toward them. At the age of 51, Abraham Lincoln was elected the 16th president of the United States.

Motivation from Others

Sometimes our motivation is sparked by the example of others. Many times, we do our best when we have someone to inspire us. Sandra Day O'Connor, the first female Supreme Court justice, was inspired by her mother, who worked hard to give her daughter a good education while living out in the deserts of Arizona, in a house with no running water or electricity.

Positive role models can inspire you to succeed.

While we know that true motivation comes from within, other people can encourage us to find that motivation within ourselves. We often find ourselves working harder when we receive positive feedback from other people. An instructor or supervisor who lets us know we are doing a good job inspires us to do even better.

When it seems, though, that there are few people around to cheer us on, we know we can provide the voice inside us that says, "You are doing great!"

S C E N E

6–2

⌒

D I A N E ' S   S T O R Y

Diane finds the motivation she needs.

Diane was late for the appointment with her adviser, just as her instructor could have predicted. She sat down and talked about how unfair the instructor was and how stupid she thought the rules were. She was very surprised when the adviser asked, "Diane, why did you come back to school?"

"I'm here to get my GED."

"Why do you want your GED?" she was asked.

At first, Diane didn't know what to say. Then she started to talk about how much she wanted to get a better-paying job. But what did all this have to do with being late for class?

Then the adviser remarked, "You know, for someone who wants so much to be a well-paid employee, you seem to be doing everything you can *not* to be one. Why do you think that is so?"

As they talked, Diane began to realize how afraid she was of failing. If she showed up late for her classes, she would have an excuse for her failure. She really wanted to get a good job. But what if she couldn't succeed? Looking back, Diane realized that whenever she felt nervous or afraid of failing, she would show up late. Instead of talking about her concerns, she would talk about how much she hated schedules. The adviser suggested that Diane think less about failure and think more about how much she wanted to succeed.

Diane used self-talk to help motivate herself to be on time. "I can be in class on time," and "I will leave the house 10 minutes earlier every day." Then Diane visualized herself arriving at class on time. She didn't have to worry about finding a parking place. She was relaxed as she walked into the classroom and didn't have to hurry to get out her books or find a pen to write with.

Diane's adviser told her that it was important to do something right away to work toward her goal, so she wrote a positive word picture, emphasizing what she would rather than wouldn't do. As she taped the word picture to the bathroom mirror, Diane read it again out loud. "I leave for class every morning at 7:15. This gives me enough time to allow for traffic and parking, and I can walk leisurely to class. I arrive calmly and ready to listen to the day's lesson."

As Diane began to see herself arriving on time, she was motivated to take the steps necessary to achieve her goal. It was difficult for Diane to change her routine. As she began to arrive at school earlier, she was motivated to try harder every morning. Soon Diane's instructors and friends could depend on her to be on time. Diane felt a sense of pride and accomplishment when she knew she had developed an important skill for both her personal life and her future employment.

THOUGHT-PROVOKING   QUESTIONS

1. Which is more important, personal achievement or material success? Can you have both? Can you be happy with only one? Is this a personal value?

2. What might be missing from goals that others set for you? What do you believe is the key element in goals that you set for yourself? Why?

3. Why would you want to move out of your comfort zone?

4. Write about the statement "The most important step toward your goal is the one you take *now*." Identify a goal and the steps you will need to achieve it. What one step can you take *now?*

5. "They who have conquered doubt and fear have conquered failure." What do you think this statement means? What do you think it says about failure and success? What does it say about taking risks? Is there a risk you could take right now?

Positive Self-Talk

Your desire to succeed makes you set goals and use self-discipline and self-talk to reach them. A desire to succeed is not the only factor that motivates you. Fear of failure also motivates. Another factor—fear of success—has just the opposite effect on you. Fear of success demotivates. This fear defeats any goals you may set; it causes you to resist change.

Joyce, for example, wanted to go to college to earn an Associates degree. She set the goal and made lists of tasks to make it happen. But three years later, she is still "thinking about it." Joyce wants a college education, but deep down she's afraid that getting it will change the way members of her family, who have not attended college, relate to her. They may view a college-educated Joyce as "different," maybe even "uppity."

Jerry has worked on the production line at Sunray Motors for nearly five years. His boss spoke with him about being a line foreman. Jerry wanted to go for the promotion and was pretty sure he could learn the new skills the foreman's job requires. After 18 months, though, Jerry is still on the line. One of his buddies from Line C is now his boss, promoted to foreman about three months ago. Jerry wanted the job, but deep down he was afraid he'd lose his friends at work if he tried to be their boss.

Instructions:

1. *Do you know anyone who seems to fear success like Joyce and Jerry in the examples? If so, on the first line below, list the person's first name only and describe the situation. Then write what you think the person may fear. Lines are provided for more examples.*

_____ _____ _____

_____ _____ _____

_____ _____ _____

_____ _____ _____

_____ _____ _____

_____ _____ _____

_____ _____ _____

2. *Now consider whether a fear of success may be keeping you from making some of the changes you've said you were going to make. Describe your situation(s) below; try to pinpoint the specific fear.*

_____

_____

_____

_____

_____

_____

3. *The negative statements that follow may reflect a fear of success. Can you turn each one into a positive statement that would help you overcome that fear?*

Negative: I don't know where to begin.

Positive: _____

Negative: I can't help it; that's just the way I am.

Positive: _____

Negative: I don't think it'll work.

Positive: _____

Negative: I'll never make it big at anything.

Positive: _____

Negative: With my luck . . .

Positive: _____

Negative: Nobody tells me anything . . .

Positive: _____

Negative: She (He) has an "in" with the boss; that leaves me out.

Positive: _____

Negative: Nobody ever gave me a break.

Positive: _____

Negative: I'd show them (employer) what I can do if they'd ever give me a chance.

Positive: _____

Negative: I'd do better if I didn't have to do everybody else's work.

Positive: _____

Negative: Who wants to get ahead in a place like this!

Positive: _____

Negative: I can't decide what's the best way to go.

Positive: _____

Negative: I'll always be limited in what I can do—my health, you know.

Positive: _____

Negative: Who can meet their unreasonable requirements?

Positive: _____

Negative: People don't like me; I intimidate them.

Positive: _____

4.   *Review what you wrote for Step 2. Does your fear of success involve any negative self-talk? Make a list of those negative statements on the lines below.*

Negative: _____

Positive: _____

Negative: _____

Positive: _____

Negative: _____

Positive: _____

Negative: _____

Positive: _____

5.   *Repeat Step 3 on the negative statements you just listed.*

Standing Your Ground

Don't allow others to add negative self-talk to your thinking. Remember, words have power. The negative words of others can undercut your esteem-building efforts unless you're ready to stand your ground. Standing your ground in this case involves responding to negatives with positives. Just as you now counter your own negative self-talk with positive thoughts and actions, you can counter others' words. Become familiar with the skill of standing your ground in this activity. Then make a point of practicing it whenever you are unavoidably in the presence of a person who thinks, talks, and acts negatively.[*]

1. *Consider each negative statement that follows and how you could respond to it in a positive way. Write your word-for-word response in the space provided.*

    Example:

    – *Statement:*   *We'll never meet this deadline.*

    + *Response:*   *We can do it with teamwork.*

    – Statement: You'll never pass that exam; it's too hard.

    + Response: _____

    – Statement: That new instructor is so mean; she doesn't like anybody.

    + Response: _____

    – Statement: Who wants to take a walk in this awful weather?

    + Response: _____

    – Statement: Everybody's applying for that part-time job. You don't have a chance.

    + Response: _____

    – Statement: We'll never be able to do that assignment and still have time to go to the beach this weekend.

    + Response: _____

[*]Note: Reinforce the Winner mentality by choosing friends and associates who build you up with their positive outlook. Choose reading material, television programs, and music that helps you feel good about yourself, too. Winners are choosy.

2. *With another student who has completed Step 1, go through the list of statements together. Start by taking the role of the negative speaker while the other student returns her or his positive responses. Then reverse roles. (This exercise will help you to see that each state-ment can be answered more than one way—all of them positive.) Repeat Step 2 if time permits, trying to respond naturally, rather than reading from your list.*

3. *Describe how you felt when you stood your ground against the battery of negative statements.*

    _____

    _____

    _____

4. *Can you recall a negative statement someone said to you within the past 24 hours? If so, write the statement and your response below:*

    Statement   _____

    Response   _____

5. *Did you stand your ground?*

    ☐   Yes, I answered a negative statement with a positive response.
    ☐   No, I "went along" with the speaker, adding another negative statement.
    ☐   Not sure; I probably could have responded more positively than I did.

6. *If you did not check yes in Step 5, consider how you might have responded. If you were in that same situation again, what would you say?*

    _____

7. *Try to monitor your conversations in the next couple of days. Make a list of negative statements spoken to you and your response to each of them. (If you did not respond positively, write what you might have said in that space.)*

    – Statement: _____

    + Response: _____

    – Statement: _____

    + Response: _____

    – Statement: _____

    + Response: _____

    – Statement: _____

    + Response: _____

8. *How frequently did you actually give a positive response to a negative statement?*

☐ Always
☐ Sometimes
☐ Rarely
☐ Never

9. *How is standing your ground like positive self-talk? Explain how you think the factors work together and why it's important for you to practice both.*

_____

_____

_____

10. *Are you using the positive self-talk statement you created in Activity 4–4? Check the item that fits you.*

☐ Yes, I read my card aloud every morning and night at home.

☐ Yes, I carry my card with me and read it several times a day.

☐ Yes, I forget only now and then, but I always go back to it the next day.

☐ Yes, I'm ready to revise my self-talk statement.

☐ No, I haven't practiced self-talk, but I'll turn to the directions on p. 151 right NOW.

If you checked any yes item in this step, go to step 11.

11. *Describe the value of using a self-talk statement. Do it in just one word.*

Write your answer here: _____

Personal Motivation

Motivation is a force within you that drives you. It is not a mysterious force, however, that moves in and takes over. You choose to have high motivation that leads you "upward and onward" toward your goals, or low motivation that leads you in another direction, away from your goals. Your use of the activities in this book shows that you intend to be driven (by motivation) toward your goals.

If you have an appointment in a distant city, you turn the car in the proper direction as you begin the trip. As you drive, you do everything needed to stay on the proper course. You may turn left or right; leave a two-lane road to enter an interstate highway; stop to fill the gas tank and check a map. The point is this: A good start and good intentions will not get you there; only continuous driving in the right direction will.

The same is true of motivation. Choose now to do whatever it takes to keep your driving force headed the way you want it to go. This activity is for refueling. Use it now and then to remind yourself where you've been and where you're going.

Instructions:

1. *Finish each of the following statements:*

    a. I am confident that _____

    b. I like doing _____

    c. I am learning _____

    d. I want to _____

    e. I like _____

    f. I know I can _____

    g. I can see problems ahead but _____

    h. I can help someone _____

    i. I am really good at _____

    j. I am interested in _____

    k. I am curious about _____

    l. I want to travel to _____

2. *What will your age be in 12 years?* _____

3. *Imagine that you are now that age (Step 2) and finish these statements again.*

   a. I like doing _____

   b. I am learning _____

   c. I want to _____

   d. I can see problems ahead but _____

   e. I can help someone _____

   f. I am interested in _____

4. *Imagine that you are observing your 80th birthday. After blowing out the candles on your birthday cake, you pause a few minutes to reflect on an earlier time—this time, the days you are living right now. What do you remember?*

   _____

   _____

   _____

   _____

5. *Think back to when you were eight years old. What do you remember from that year of your life?*

   _____

   _____

   _____

   _____

   _____

6. *In Step 5, are most of your memories happy (positive) or unhappy (negative)?* _____

   Do you agree or disagree with the statement that people tend to remember only the good things?

   _____ *Explain:* _____

   _____

   _____

   _____

   _____

Success at Work

Most adults spend much of their time and energy working. Getting and keeping jobs and planning a career take up a large part of life. Work, on-the-job relationships, and career achievements are also potential sources of much satisfaction in life. Yet, some people see work as drudgery—a daily grind. As in every other area of your life, how you view work—and yourself as a worker—is a choice. Activity 6–4 is designed to help you focus on your attitude and actions concerning your work.

This textbook is about success. What is success? Is success making lots of money? Is it a high-level position? Or do you believe that success is happiness? Success is feeling good about yourself.

_____

Instructions:

> *If you have a part-time job, or if you do volunteer work, think of this job as a permanent, full-time assignment. If you do not have a job now, put yourself in the place of someone close to you who is employed (a parent, spouse, or friend).*

1. *What do you really want out of work? Think about it. Nobody else can decide for you—certainly not your employer. What do YOU want?*

   _____   _____   _____

   _____   _____   _____

   _____   _____   _____

   _____   _____   _____

2. *Write down every one of your desires, dreams, and goals (use a separate sheet if you need more space). Include subjects you want to learn, skills you want to acquire, places you want to visit, hobbies you want to pursue, things you want to own. See Activity 6–3 and Dream Job (Activity 3–4). Whether it's financial, mental, physical, or spiritual, writing it is important. A maker of little office bulletin boards used the slogan, "A short note is better than a long memory." Make it your slogan. Write it; remember it.*

   _____   _____   _____

   _____   _____   _____

   _____   _____   _____

   _____   _____   _____

_____ _____ _____

_____ _____ _____

_____ _____ _____

_____ _____ _____

_____ _____ _____

_____ _____ _____

3. *Out of the list of goals (Step 2), pick five that are most important to you. Write the five goals on the lines at left below.*

Goals   *Actions*

_____   _____

                                                 _____

                                                 _____

_____   _____

                                                 _____

                                                 _____

                                                 _____

_____   _____

                                                 _____

                                                 _____

_____   _____

                                                 _____

                                                 _____

_____   _____

                                                 _____

                                                 _____

4. *Now, beside each of the goals listed in Step 3, write three actions you can take right now toward reaching that goal. "A BIG SUCCESS is simply several little successes linked together."* (Consider the problems you can answer for others, what needs of theirs you can fill.)*

*Mike Murdock, *Wisdom and Inspiration for Today's Business Professional* (Tulsa, Oklahoma: Honor Books, 1992), p. 199.

5. *On the following list, check (✓) items that you currently practice on the job; put an ✗ by the things you do not do.*

_____   a. View work as pleasant, enjoyable, and satisfying.

_____   b. Do work that fits your abilities and interests.

_____   c. Learn as much as you can about your job.

_____   d. Return a "full day's work for a full day's pay."

_____   e. Keep a daily to-do list of on-the-job tasks.

_____   f. Set deadlines in addition to any that are set for you.

_____   g. Use criticism to your advantage.

_____   h. Ask the boss how you can do your job better.

_____   i. Admit your mistakes and make needed corrections.

_____   j. Ask for help from your boss as needed.

_____   k. Ask for supplies or equipment that you need.

_____   l. Help others in their responsibilities when possible.

_____   m. Refuse to spread gossip about co-workers.

_____   n. Do more than is expected of you.

_____   o. Keep accurate records.

_____   p. Write down complex and little-used procedures.

_____   q. Set your own quality standards for evaluating your work.

_____   r. Give attention to details of your work.

_____   s. Take time for self-renewal (30-second pauses at work and mini-vacations on weekends).

_____   t. Do tasks that count; never hide behind busywork.

_____   u. Look for ways to improve the quality and/or quantity of your output.

_____   v. Keep your personal data sheet (résumé) up-to-date, recording relevant information as it happens.

_____ w. Keep a "feel good" file—a collection of uplifting notes, phone messages, clippings, awards, certificates, and so on—that you can sort through whenever you have a "bad day."

_____ x. Read books or magazine articles about your employment field.

6. *From the ✓'d items (Step 5), select six. For each item selected, write a sentence beginning with the words, This work trait shows that, as an employee, I am* _____.

Example: Do tasks that count; never hide behind busywork.

This work trait shows that, as an employee, I am effective and productive and valuable to my employer.

✓'d item: _____
This work trait shows that, as an employee, I am

_____.

✓'d item: _____
This work trait shows that, as an employee, I am

_____.

✓'d item: _____
This work trait shows that, as an employee, I am

_____.

✓'d item: _____
This work trait shows that, as an employee, I am

_____.

✓'d item: _____
This work trait shows that, as an employee, I am

_____.

✓'d item: _____
This work trait shows that, as an employee, I am

_____.

7. *Review the ✗'d items (Step 2). Select the three that appeal to you most and that you can try immediately. Write your choices below. Under each item, complete the sentence that begins, Taking this action at work will help me to* _____. *(For now, ignore the numbered spaces under each item.)*

✗'d item: _____

Taking this action at work will help me to _____

    1. _____

    2. _____

    3. _____

✗'d item: _____

Taking this action at work will help me to _____

    1. _____

    2. _____

    3. _____

✗'d item: _____

Taking this action at work will help me to _____

    1. _____

    2. _____

    3. _____

8. *If any item in Step 7 must be done in steps, rather than all at once, make a list of those steps in the numbered spaces under the item.*

Positive Projection

Remember the activity titled Admire a Hero (Activity 3–3)? In it, you were advised to study someone whom you admire very much and decide why you prize her or him. You tend to mimic the qualities of a person you respect greatly. By analyzing the person's qualities, you make those traits easier to imitate.

As a child, you had heroes all around you, including those in books, on TV, and in the movies. Perhaps you remember thinking, When I grow up I want to be just like _____.

That simple idea can still work for you in your adult life. If an eight-year-old can project (look forward in time) to "when I grow up," a person of any age can project to a later time. In this activity, you will project. You're not trying to become that person, and you certainly don't want to diminish your own strong qualities. In positive projection, you're simply naming another tool to keep you motivated. The purpose of this activity is to help you identify the qualities that you admire in others so that you can develop those same qualities more fully in yourself.

1. *Think of people you know well who are at least 10 years older than you. Jot down their first names or initials below.*

_____   _____   _____

_____   _____   _____

_____   _____   _____

_____   _____   _____

_____   _____   _____

_____   _____   _____

_____   _____   _____

2. *Circle the name of persons on your list who are the same gender (man or woman) as you.*

3. *Think about the men or women whose names you've circled. Pick the individual whom you most admire or respect—the one you'd want to be like when you're his or her age. Write the name or initials below.*

_____

4. *What makes this person special? What qualities made him or her stand out from the crowd? Think for five full minutes and list all the qualities that come to mind.*

_____   _____   _____

_____   _____   _____

_____   _____   _____

_____   _____   _____

_____   _____   _____

5. *Go over the list of qualities (Step 4). Do you have any of these qualities? Put a ✓to the right of those traits the two of you have in common. You will want to keep these qualities and make them ever stronger.*

6. *Which traits in Step 5 would you need to work on to become more like the person you admire? Put a ✓to the left of those items.*

7. *Write a sentence to be added to your positive self-talk statement (3" x 5" card) the next time you read it. If you prefer, use the following sentence with the blank filled in. Every day of my life, I am becoming more and more _____ (insert one or two of the qualities checked in Step 6). If you carry your card with you, add the sentence to it now.*

8. *In this space, create a word picture of the person you will be in 10 years (or whenever you reach the age of the special person named in Step 3). Project your appearance, attitude, values, and so on. Describe the great person you will be in rich detail.*

_____

_____

_____

_____

_____

_____

_____

_____

_____

_____

_____

Great minds have purposes, others have wishes.

Washington Irving

Psychology of Self-Direction

After you have read this chapter and completed the activities, you will:

- Be able to set specific and clearly defined goals.

- Be able to apply new strategies for dealing with problems.

- Be able to manage your time and set priorities.

- Be able to look at your budget and keep track of your expenses.

- See that happiness comes in working toward and reaching new goals.

SCENE

7–1

J A S O N ' S   S T O R Y

"Where do I go from here?"

Jason is working toward becoming a computer technician. His grades
are good, but he struggles with the cost of going to school. Jason is
married, and his wife's job pays most of their bills while he is going
to school. When he enrolled, he went to the financial aid office at his
school and applied for a student loan. When he found that he had
been approved for the loan, he was really excited. Jason is confident
that he will be able to find a good job, but he just learned that his wife
is pregnant with their first baby. How will he manage all those
payments? Jason feels confused and unsure.

"I thought applying for the loan was a lot of work; now I have to pay
it all back," he worried. "I only have six months after graduation
before I have to start making payments. I want to pay it all back, but I
don't see how I can afford it and everything else as well. Especially
since we won't be able to count on Sally's income for several months.
I thought I would be all set after graduation. Now I feel like I have a
whole new set of problems. Where do I go from here? Help!"

What can Jason do?

Dr. Waitley focuses on self-direction and how it can help us establish short- and long-term goals, manage our time, and form a future life plan.

⤜ *What Is Self-Direction?*

Self-direction is setting a well-defined goal and working toward it. Most people spend more time planning a party, studying the newspaper, or making a holiday list than they spend planning their lives. Winners set their daily goals the afternoon or evening before. They list on paper at least six tasks to do tomorrow. The next day, they check off tasks as they accomplish them. They carry over to the following day's plan the tasks not completed and new ones just added.

Winners set goals for themselves to give direction to their lives.

Can you imagine if you did your grocery shopping without a list? What if you went down to the supermarket without a plan, to sort of "play it by ear"? You would see all the displays advertised on TV, hundreds of irresistible goodies—the latest in miracle scrubbing bubbles and delectable delights. You could be overwhelmed by items you didn't know about, didn't need, and didn't really want. You went to the supermarket for lettuce, tomatoes, and other ingredients for a nice salad, but since you didn't write it down you might come home with things you don't need.

The mind is like a computer and needs specific instructions to operate. The reason most people don't reach their goals is that they don't define them, learn about them, or seriously consider them believable or achievable. In other words, they never *set* their goals.

Winners can tell you where they are going, what they plan to do along the way, and who will be sharing their adventure with them. Winners in life—those one-in-a-hundred people—set themselves apart from the rest by an important trait they develop: self-direction. They have a game plan for life. Every Winner figures out where he or she is going day by day, every day. Winners are goal- and role-oriented. They set goals and get what they want. They direct themselves along the road to fulfillment.

☞ *Who Are the Winners?*

Winners are those individuals who, in a very natural, free-flowing way, seem to consistently get what they want out of life. They put themselves together across the board—in their personal, professional, and community lives. They set and achieve goals that benefit others as well as themselves.

You don't have to get lucky to win at life, and you don't have to knock down other people or gain at the expense of others. Winning is taking the talent or potential you were born with and have since developed and using it fully toward a purpose that makes you feel worthwhile according to your own standards.

Winners look for opportunities to make their own good luck.

Seeking goals is like using a homing torpedo system. This system constantly monitors feedback from a set target area. The torpedo system adjusts the course setting in its computer. It makes all necessary adjustments to stay on target and score a hit. If the system is programmed incorrectly or aimed at a target out of range, the homing torpedo will wander around until its system fails or it self-destructs.

So it is with everyone. Set a goal and this homing system adjusts the self-image setting to make decisions for reaching goals. If it is programmed with goals that are not realistic or well thought out, the human system will wander aimlessly until it wears itself out or self-destructs.

☞ *A Purpose in Life*

Winners are people with a definite purpose in life. Dr. Viktor Frankl was a psychiatrist in Vienna in the 1930s and became a prisoner in Nazi prison camps during World War II. He experienced three years of horror at Dachau and Auschwitz, narrowly escaping the gas chamber and death several times. In his book, *Man's Search for Meaning,* Frankl used his experience and observations in the camps to write about human behavior under extreme conditions. Movies and television dramatizations such as *Schindler's List* and *Holocaust* remind us of this human suffering.

Seeing himself and others stripped of everything—their families, jobs, clothing, possessions, health, dignity—Frankl studied the behavior of the captives. He wrote down the facts without letting his emotions interfere. He noticed that the captives, who faced the possibility of death every day, were able to survive starvation and torture if they felt they had a purpose for living. Those who felt they had no reason for staying alive died quickly and easily. The ones who lived through the death camps were nearly all individuals who had a fierce determination to see a loved one or do something important in their lives.

More than any other authority on human behavior, Frankl based his knowledge on firsthand experience. His observations are very different from Sigmund Freud's. Freud said that people may look different but that if they were all deprived of food, they would all behave the same. He felt they would all descend to their basic animal-like instincts.

When Frankl witnessed two people faced with the identical situation in the concentration camps, he saw one crumble and give up while the other stayed strong and hopeful. He saw that people may react in very different ways to the same situation, depending on their inner drive and motivation. Many prisoners told Frankl that they no longer expected anything of life. Frankl pointed out that they had it backward. He said, "Life was expecting something of them. Life asks of every individual to discover what it should be."

Winners have an inner drive and motivation that give purpose to their lives.

Purpose is what enables each of us to face up to difficult times and tragedies in our lives.

Where there is life, there is hope.

Where there are hopes, there are dreams.

Where there are vivid dreams, repeated, there are goals.

What Are Goals?

A **goal** is the outcome you want and toward which you direct all your effort. Goals become the game plans that Winners focus on in great detail. They know that inner commitment makes achievement happen. What kinds of goals are you committed to? Since we become what we think about most, we are unconsciously moving toward the achievement of the thoughts we are having right now. Negative attitudes create negative goals; positive attitudes create positive goals.

Winners use self-discipline to focus on well-defined goals.

We all have the potential and the opportunity for success in our lives. It takes just as much energy for a bad life as it does for a good life. So many of us lead unhappy aimless lives, existing from day to day and year to year, confused, frustrated, and in a prison of our own making. We can set ourselves free by deciding what to do with our lives, by making goals happen.

Rather than being like a ship without a rudder, drifting helplessly until we end up on the rocks, we can discipline ourselves to decide where we want to go. We can chart a course and sail straight and far, reaching one port after another. We can accomplish more in just a few years than others accomplish in a lifetime.

We can do it by picturing our goals. Think of a long ocean voyage halfway around the world. Even though the captain of the ship cannot *see* his destination for most of the journey, he knows what it is, where it is, and that he will reach it if he keeps following the right course.

Lifetime Goals

Winners in life start with lifetime goals. They have a two-year plan. A one-year program. A six-month campaign. A summer project. They set their priorities and through self-direction they work to reach them. They set a clearly defined goal, write it down, and dwell on it morning and night as if they had already achieved it. They assemble support materials—news articles, books, tapes, pictures cut out of magazines—anything that can help them see their goals.

Review your goals with Winners and experts who have accomplished what you want to and who are genuinely willing to help you. One of the best ways is to pay someone for her time and expert knowledge to give you advice for pursuing your goals in life.

Happiness

Happiness is a state of well-being and contentment that comes from living a worthwhile life. It is not a goal to chase after. Happiness is the natural experience of winning your own self-respect and the respect of others. Happiness should not be confused with indulging yourself, escaping something, or pleasure seeking. You cannot inhale, drink, or smoke happiness. You cannot buy it, wear it, drive it, swallow it, inject it, or travel to it. Happiness is the journey, not the destination.

Winners are happy when they work hard toward achieving their goals.

We become that which we think about the most. Remember, no wind blows in favor of a ship without a rudder. The person without a purpose is like a ship without a rudder.

Get behind the helm. Plan the work and work the plan, one day at a time. Decide now on your goals, and work constantly to make those goals take root in your subconscious. See yourself achieving those goals one by one. Make winning your game plan for life and win today!

WIN

Let's take a closer look at some of the points Dr. Waitley discussed and learn how to use the principle of self-direction in our everyday lives.

The Importance of Self-Direction

Self-direction means setting a clear goal and working toward it. Dr. Waitley calls it a "game plan for life," and talks about the importance of knowing where you are going each day, every day. As the saying goes, "If you fail to plan, you plan to fail."

Experts tell us that the more specific and detailed you can be about setting a goal, the better. Rather than saying, "I will save money," it is more constructive to say, "I will save $200 this year." Phrasing your goal in a specific and concrete way makes it easier to focus on.

Short-Term and Long-Term Goals

There are two types of goals: short-term and long-term. Short-term goals have a short time frame. They are the things you are working on today, tomorrow, next week. Long-term goals are further in the future. They are the goals you want to accomplish in a few weeks, a month, a year, or several years. Many long-term goals are actually several smaller short-term goals. For instance, let's say your long-term goal is to get a B in your accounting course. Your short-term goals might be to study for an hour each day and to score well on the next three exams. Your successful smaller goals lead to the success of the larger goal. It is easy to think of large goals as the "important" ones, but small, everyday goals are just as important. Meeting our smaller goals sets us on the path to bigger successes.

Short-term goals are important building blocks toward reaching a larger long-term goal.

Long-term goals are the major targets in your life. Long-term goals can include things like continuing your education, saving up to buy a house, or beginning a career in your field of interest. Long-term goals can require a lot of patience, but it is worth it in the end. Ask yourself at the end of every day what you have done to bring yourself closer to your goals.

Examine your long-term goal to break it down into achievable, productive, short-term pieces.

Make sure your daily activities tie in to your longer-term goals and values. A daily plan should reflect the "big picture" in your life plan. Likewise, a yearly plan should be broken down into daily, weekly, and monthly activities. For example, if your goal this year is to become physically fit, your monthly plan might be to improve your heart rate. Your weekly plan would be to include three or more days of aerobic exercise. Your daily plan would be to take the stairs instead of the elevator and to eat sensible meals. Your daily, weekly, and monthly targets relate directly to your larger life goal.

In *Why Some Positive Thinkers Get Powerful Results*, Norman Vincent Peale talks about setting major goals and achieving them by listing nine steps:

1.   Think about where you want to go in life.
2.   Come to a firm decision about your basic goal.
3.   Write down your goal in a clear statement.
4.   Study and learn all you can about your goal.
5.   Set a time for achieving your goal.
6.   Make sure your decision about your goal is right.
7.   Give your goal all your effort and never stop trying.
8.   Be a positive thinker.
9.   Once you have achieved one goal, go on to the next.

Dr. Peale talks about using a technique to keep your goals close at hand. Write each goal on a small card and carry them in your pocket. Each time you think of another goal, write it down on a card and add it to the others in your pocket. As you achieve your goals, remove the cards. Take the cards out and read them to remind yourself of all the successes you are working toward.

Dealing with Problems

Working toward goals will involve overcoming problems when they arise. We have to see ourselves as bigger and stronger than any problem. Positive self-talk is a great tool for helping us to take responsibility for solving our problems. Here are some examples of self-talk that can help us get through the rough spots:

Use positive self-talk to give you confidence to solve your problems.

•   I am good at solving problems. I like challenges and meet them head-on.
•   Problems are my teachers. They help me learn and grow.
•   There is no problem I cannot conquer.
•   I don't fear problems; I solve them.

Instead of being sidetracked by the problem, we need to keep the vision of success clearer than ever. Take charge of the problem and accept responsibility for solving it. Remember, though, that when problems arise we don't always have to fight them alone. Call on your support system when problems seem overwhelming. Winners are not afraid to ask for help. They know that next time they will be doing the helping!

"If only" lets your problem control you. You take control!

It's important not to fall into a trap of saying "if only." We need to determine the facts of the problem, be aware of options we have to solve it, and tackle it one step at a time.

Fact.   You have to write three papers for your English class this term. You want to turn in professional-looking papers and earn good grades. You do not have a computer, word processor, or typewriter but do not want to turn in a handwritten paper. Do you say, "If only I had a computer, I could . . . "? No, you look at your options instead.

Options.   Buy new equipment. Borrow or use equipment that belongs to a friend or relative. Use equipment in a computer lab at school. Use equipment at the public library.

Tackle the Problem One Step at a Time.   If you can afford it, you might decide to shop for new equipment. Some stores offer payment plans that may fit into your budget. You will need to determine what your budget will allow and then choose the equipment accordingly. If there is no money for new equipment, ask your friends or relatives if they have equipment you may use. You might want to offer to do a favor for them in return. Still no luck? Check the schedule at the computer lab at school. Be sure you can have your papers written before open lab times. Sign up for specific times or plan to arrive early if equipment is on a first-come, first-served basis. No equipment available or the network "down"? Public libraries often have equipment that you may rent on an hourly basis. If for some reason you still aren't able to prepare your paper, go to your instructor. Be prepared to list the steps you've already taken and then ask for advice.

☞ Time Management

Time management is an important part of reaching goals. We can budget our time as we do our money and set aside time for school, family, job, and other obligations. Some days, of course, we have to spend more time in one area than another. Try keeping a weekly calendar, writing down all the important things you need to do. This will allow you to see how well you are using your time. You may find a new way to rearrange your schedule that allows you more time for work and fun. Also, a calendar can remind you of important appointments and keep you on time for them.

Keeping a daily schedule can also be helpful. Write down your activities in a typical day and ask yourself the following questions:

Keep track of your time and you may find some extra.

- Do I have time to do what I want to do?
- How much free time do I have each day?
- Where am I wasting time?
- Where can I use my time better?
- Am I trying to do a million things at once?
- Am I making enough time for relaxation and fun after I get my work done?
- Is my schedule the same every day?

These questions are a valuable tool to help you organize your day better. Sometimes it seems as though there are too many things to do and never enough time. If you still cannot find the time you need after taking a close look at your routine, try asking an instructor or counselor for advice. One of them will help you organize your time in the best and most efficient way.

Handling Big Projects

Writing down the things you have to do can help you break down big projects into smaller tasks. For example, let's say you have to write a paper for your technical writing class that is due on Friday afternoon. Since this is too big a project to do all at once, you could divide your tasks as follows:

Big projects are like long-term goals. Break a big project into smaller steps.

Monday:	Go to the library and get information on the topic.
Tuesday:	Read through the information you found and prepare an outline.
Wednesday:	Write a rough draft. Revise and edit your paper.
Thursday:	Key, proofread, and print the final draft.
Friday:	Relax!

You might be thinking, "That project took all week. I don't want to drag things out like that!" Yes, if you did the project this way, it would take four days. However, you would be working only a couple of hours each day. You wouldn't get tired and frustrated the way you would if you tried to do the whole project in one day. Your classmates who had put the assignment off would have to work all day Friday—researching, writing notes, and typing the paper. Because you did a little bit of the project each day, you are all done, and the weekend's begun.

Punctuality

Another part of time management is breaking the lateness habit. Your weekly calendar will help you in this. Decide to be early for appointments. When you have somewhere to go, determine what time you need to arrive. Then figure out how long it will take to get ready and to travel there. Count backwards and you will know what time you must start to get ready. Include an extra 5 to 10 minutes to arrive early for appointments. This is especially true for job interviews, but is true also for showing up to classes and work every day. You may need those extra minutes to allow for possible traffic problems and weather conditions. Winners show up on time because they know that time is valuable. Also, they don't want to miss anything.

Allow yourself extra time and you will develop the punctuality habit.

Money Management

We have seen how you can budget your time. When you also budget your money, you can use your money more wisely and use it as needed to achieve your goals. For students, affording school is a major goal. Schools have financial aid offices to assist students and their families in meeting the cost of education, and students can choose from many different financial packages. Money may be available from grants and scholarships to help pay for college tuition. Another option may be to borrow money from banks or other institutions.

Many schools offer work-study programs and part-time employment opportunities for students to work their way through school. Some students may be eligible for educational assistance from a variety of agencies and programs.

Creating a budget is the first step in controlling your money. A budget is the plan necessary to control the incoming and outgoing money for saving and spending. Experts agree that it is helpful to sit down and make a chart of your finances—how much money is coming in, and how much is going out. Try making a copy of the chart for each month so that you get a detailed look at your financial situation. When you can pinpoint unnecessary expenses, you can decide on a new spending plan and use that "found" money in a way that will help you achieve your goals. You might put money aside to pay for child care, car repairs, or books. After you graduate, you might save for a new wardrobe or start paying off student loans.

If you have access to a computer, there is a variety of money management software available to help you prepare your budget and analyze your spending. These software programs also allow you to keep a computerized checkbook register to use for reconciling your account each month when your bank statement arrives.

Self-Direction and Happiness

Self-direction can help you set goals, manage your time and money, and organize your life. When you accomplish these things, will you be happy? Let's take a look at what happiness means.

Personal Happiness

Dr. Waitley talked about the idea of happiness as a state of contentment and well-being. The psychologist William James called happiness "the secret motive that drives everyone." In the 1970s, psychologists began to study the idea of happiness, what it means, and how it is achieved. The magazine *Psychology Today* ran the first of many "happiness surveys" in 1975.

Most people consider personal happiness the most important thing in their lives. People also tend to think that success and happiness are the same thing. They think, "When I am successful, I will be happy." Most people want success. Yet sometimes people spend so much time and energy trying to be successful that they forget about being happy in smaller ways in their everyday lives.

Happiness is not a goal. Happiness comes when you believe you are accomplishing your goals.

The ancient Greeks defined happiness as "pleasure and control." So many of us wait for happiness to "happen" instead of creating it for ourselves. Happiness has been referred to as a by-product of a full, active life. Generally, we find that happiness is not the end result of an action but part of the process of doing it. The ancient mystics had a story to describe this point.

An old tiger observed a young tiger running frantically in circles, trying to catch his tail. "Why are you running about like that?" the old tiger asked. "Because," said the young tiger, "I have been told that happiness lies in one's tail, and I am trying to catch it." "I, too, have observed that happiness lies in one's tail," replied the older cat. "I have noticed also that when I chase my tail I cannot catch it, but when I walk along as usual it seems to follow me wherever I go."

A Look on the Bright Side

Attitude is a big factor of happiness. Earlier, we talked about how we can control our time: We can waste it or use it. Psychologists tell us that we can even choose our moods; we can choose happiness. It might not always be easy, but it can be done with a little practice. For instance, it is easy to fall into a bad mood when you wake up early and look ahead at all the tasks of the day. School, homework, job, family—it can be overwhelming. If you cannot change the tasks you have to do, though, you can change the way you feel about them. You might keep a to-do list with you and cross off each item when you get it done. You could look at the list as a challenge and promise yourself a hot cup of coffee and a television program as a reward for getting the items done.

Teach yourself to look on the bright side of things. If you get a bad grade on a test, look at it as a study guide. It is pointing out the topics you need to devote more time to. If the train or bus is late, choose to use the extra time reading a book or planning your schedule instead of getting upset. It is not always easy to keep a positive attitude, but strong self-discipline can help you do it. Go back and read Chapter 5 if you need some reminders about self-discipline.

As a philosopher once said, happiness is not necessarily doing what you like, but liking what you have to do. How happy are you?

S C E N E

7–2

J A S O N ' S   S T O R Y

Jason moves in the right direction.

Jason had received a student loan to help him get a degree. Now that graduation was drawing near, he was concerned about paying it back, especially since he hadn't found a full-time job and he and his wife were starting a family a little sooner than planned. So he went back to the financial aid office at his school and sat down with a staff member to explain his problem.

"Let's look at the facts and your options," said the financial aid officer. "First you need a budget." Jason and the adviser listed all the money coming in and going out. They used the income from Jason's part-time job as a guide until he finds a full-time job. They also figured how much Sally would be able to contribute. Fortunately, she works for a company that provides some maternity leave benefits that would help cover a few of the monthly bills. Jason also wrote down his and Sally's long-term financial goals—paying off the loan, saving for a car—and all the monthly expenses they would have. Together, Jason and the adviser worked out a budget that would let Jason pay all the bills, save a little, and even spend a few dollars each month on entertainment.

Jason now felt confident that he could pay off his loan according to a payment schedule and also work toward his and Sally's goals. Although they still had the same bills to pay, he felt in control of

the situation. He was moving in the right direction and left
the financial aid office with an optimistic attitude and a feeling
of happiness.

THOUGHT-PROVOKING QUESTIONS

1. Has anyone ever said to you, "If you do not *have* the time, *make* the time"? How do you think you can make time? Think about someone you know who is always busy and always getting things done. How do they make time?

2. The ancient Greeks defined happiness as "pleasure and control." Does this definition make sense to you? What do you think it means?

3. Dale Carnegie has said the following about happiness: "Happiness doesn't depend on outward conditions. It depends on inner conditions. It isn't what you have or who you are or where you are or what you are doing that makes you happy or unhappy. It is what you think about it." What do you think he means? Do you agree or disagree with him?

4. Imagine yourself in your later years of life. You overhear your grandchildren telling their friends about your life and accomplishments. Write down what you would like them to be saying about you.

5. Why are "if only" poor words to use when trying to solve a problem?

Procrastination

Procrastination is putting off or delaying action. People put things off for different reasons. Some procrastinate because they fear the outcome won't be perfect. They fear what they view as failure. Others fear success.

Staying motivated requires action. When you achieve a goal, even a tiny one, you're no longer motivated by that goal; but you are very motivated to try to meet the *next* one. By taking the first step, you start a cycle of achievement. If you procrastinate, the cycle does not begin.

One purpose of time management is to be sure that no goal is unmet because you can't "get around to it." As part of your time management, consider whether you may be procrastinating on important goals. (Are you using the to-do chart introduced in Activity 5–5?)

Instructions:

1. *For each area of your life listed in column A, decide what, if anything, you have been putting off and write it in column B. (Perhaps you listed goals in earlier textbook activities that you have not yet acted on. If so, list such items here.)*
2. *In column C, write what you will do today. (Write just one small step here—an action you're sure you can take before day's end.)*
3. *Write what follow-up action(s) you will take. The purpose is to break down a goal (column B) into many little goals. An example is given.*

My Procrastination Checkup

A Areas of Life	B I have been putting off…	C Today I am going to…	D My future plan is…	E Date
Example: Finances	Opening a savings account	Stop at the bank and make a deposit	To make a deposit each payday	
Attitude				
Career				
Community				
Education				
Finances				
Health				
Recreation				
Relationships				

4. *Look at the items listed in column C. Can you do all of these items today? If not, break the item into a smaller first step.*

5. *In column E, write the target date (Mo/Yr) when you expect to achieve the goal in column D. Short-term goals may be completed within a few days or weeks. Long-term goals may take months or even years. Realistic target dates will help you reach your goals. Attempting to reach a long-term goal too quickly can be a setup for failure.*

Draw a Tree

1. *In the space below, draw a tree to represent how you feel about yourself today.*

2. *Form a group with two other students in your class and explain your pictures.*

3. *How is this tree different from one you might have drawn on the first day of this course? These words may help you express it:*

bark	fruit	roots	tree house
birds	leaves	sapling	trunk
branches	limb	seedpod	twigs
forest fire	needles	soil	underbrush
forest	rain	sunshine	watered

4. *Did you enjoy this activity? _____ What, in particular, did you like or dislike about it?*

_____

_____

_____

SMART Goals

In Chapter 7, you read that a well-set goal is conceivable, believable, desirable, achievable, and measurable. An easy way to remember the aspects of a well-set goal is to associate the word SMART.

Specific   The goal is definite, or exact, not vague or open to interpretation.

Measurable   The goal is stated in terms of quantity, dimensions, or capacity; for example, amount of money saved, number of books read, total miles jogged, smaller shirt size.

Achievable   The goal can be reached successfully. A goal does not have to be easy—most are not—but it does have to be doable.

Realistic   The goal relates to things as they actually are; it's down to earth.

Time related   The goal includes a target date for reaching it.

SMART characteristics are key. A "goal" is not a goal if one of these factors is missing.

_____

Instructions:

1. *In the following list, identify which characteristic(s) is (are) missing. Write S(specific), M(measurable), A(achievable), R(realistic), and/or T(time related) in the middle column. Write OK if all of the SMART factors are present. An example is shown.*

Goal	Missing Factor	SMART Goal
Example: Read my self-talk card every day.	*S, M, T*	*Read my self-talk card aloud in front of a mirror every morning and night for 30 days.*
Ask some people this week if I can list their names as references on job application forms.		
Go with Adopt-a-Highway team every Saturday morning (9 till 12) March through November to pick up litter.		
Find out in next two weeks how to get financial aid for next quarter.		
Pay off all credit cards this month.		
Eat right three times a day for the next 10 days.		

concluded Goal	Missing Factor	SMART Goal
Work out in gym for an hour (midnight to 1 AM) three times a week.		
Call home for 10 minutes on Saturday morning or Sunday afternoon every other weekend during the school year.		
See a good movie this weekend.		
Check help wanted ads in the newspapers several times a week until school is out.		
Call by 4 PM Thursday to volunteer for this year's Neighborhood Repair Affair (8 till 4 this Saturday).		
Write papers to erase three Incompletes on record; raise grade point average to 3.8 by end of the semester.		
Ask financial adviser when my annuity account will reach $100.00 (no change in monthly deposits).		
Get annual physical exam.		
Take a two-hour nap every afternoon.		
Record birth dates of parents, grand-parents, and siblings on a calendar, along with a reminder to send a card and handwritten note five days prior.		

2.   In the right-hand column, rewrite each goal to include the missing factors.

3.   Check your goals for SMART. Write personal goals in the left-hand column below. (Suggestion: Review completed activities in this book, selecting goals you set earlier.)

Goal	Missing Factor	SMART Goal

4. *Repeat Steps 1 and 2 on your goal statements.*

5. *Do you think SMART will help you with your goals? Explain.*

_____

_____

_____

_____

_____

Look Who's Making Headlines

Keep yourself motivated by using your imagination. Form an image of future events and put yourself in the picture. Watch each day as you move gradually from here and now to then and there. This activity involves you in visualizing an event in your future. Imagine that you have just achieved a long-term goal. Your accomplishment is to be written up in the main newspaper in your area.

1. *Take a goal you want to achieve sometime in the future. (If you completed Activity 6–4, choose one of the goals listed there.)*

2. *Write the newspaper article about your accomplishment. Remember, the readers of this future edition don't know you. Tell them who you are, where you live, how you decided on your goal, and how you reached it. A press release form is provided for your use. Write the city, state, and date of the article in this space.*

IM4ME

News Release for Release: _____

Contact: _____

Phone: _____

(* _____)

Headline:

Story:

3. *The article is accompanied by a photograph of you. Describe it. Is it a recent photo? How do you look? What are you doing?*

_____

_____

_____

_____

_____

It's About Time!*

Have you been using the to-do chart (Activity 5–5) regularly? If so, you have discovered the advantages of weekly planning. This activity will expand the to-do chart idea. It involves a procrastination worksheet and putting priorities on tasks.

Instructions:

1. _In the list below, check (✓) any items that you believe are benefits of planning your time and making a chart. Space is provided for you to add advantages that you have discovered._

_____   Keeps you from worrying about tasks before you tackle them.

_____   Helps you separate important from unimportant tasks.

_____   Helps you complete tasks on time.

_____   Keeps you motivated as you finish a task and go to the next one.

_____   Helps you balance leisure time and work.

_____   Lowers your stress level; helps you relax.

_____   Helps you use even one or two minutes for something worthwhile.

_____   Helps you pace yourself; prevents "peaks and valleys" in your activity.

_____   Helps to prevent procrastination.

_____

_____

_____

_____

_____

_____

*Adapted from _It's About Time_ by Ken Smith, Copyright 1992. Used with permission by Good News Publishers/Crossway Books, 1300 Crescent St., Wheaton, IL.

2. *On the procrastination worksheet, list things you have been putting off in the left-hand column.*

Procrastination Worksheet		
Areas of Procrastination	Priority	
	A-C-B	*1-3-2*
1		
2		
3		
4		
5		
6		
7		
8		
9		
10		
11		
12		

3. *For each item listed on the worksheet (Step 2), set a priority using the following procedure:*

   a. Identify the items that will relieve the most pressure, or stress, in your life. Mark an A in the A-C-B column beside these items.
   b. Next, identify the items that will relieve the least pressure. Mark a C beside these items.
   c. Now, write B beside the remaining items.
   d. Look at the A items only. Identify the A items that are most important; mark a 1 in the 1-3-2 column beside these A items.
   e. Repeat Step d for all B items.
   f. Finally, repeat Step d for all C items.

   The priority columns indicate the order for dealing with the areas of procrastination (A1, B1, A2, C1, A3, B2, C2, B3, C3).

4. *Refer to your procrastination worksheet and your class schedule and calendar. Then write on the daily to-do list those tasks that you must do and those you would like to plan to do today. (Many people prepare the daily to-do list in the evening for the next day. Others like to begin their day by making the to-do list.)*

Daily To-Do List			
Things to Do Today	Priority		
	A-C-B	1-3-2	✓
1			
2			
3			
4			
5			
6			
7			
8			
9			
10			
11			
12			

5. *Set priorities on the list (Step 4) as directed in Step 3. Do things in the order of priority. Check each item off when it is done. Items that you don't complete today go on tomorrow's daily to-do list. (Use blank paper to create additional daily to-do lists and procrastination worksheets.)*

6. *With a weekly list of things to do, you can write a daily to-do list very quickly.*

7. *Refer again to your procrastination worksheet, class schedule, and so on. List the things you do not need to do today but that should be done sometime this week. Set priorities as before. When you make your next daily to-do list, look here for the next highest priority items.*

Weekly To-Do List			
Things to Do This Week	Priority		
	A-C-B	1-3-2	✓
1			
2			
3			
4			
5			
6			
7			
8			
9			
10			
11			
12			

What would you attempt to do if you knew you could not fail?

Dr. Robert Schuller

Psychology of Self-Projection

CHAPTER OBJECTIVES

After you read this chapter and complete the activities, you will:

- Be able to work to make good things happen.

- Think positively.

- Project more confidence and higher self-esteem.

- Be able to use good communication skills.

- Be able to present yourself as a Winner.

S C E N E

8–1

⌒

S H E I L A ' S   S T O R Y

"What's the use?"

Sheila was very nervous. The school placement office had arranged this job interview for her at the Rolling Hills Nursing Home. She was applying for a position as nurse's aide.

Sheila was a good student and had done very well in her classes as well as her co-op experience. She really liked working with the residents and felt a sense of satisfaction whenever she was able to make someone feel a little more comfortable.

Working with the residents was sure a lot different from a job interview. She knew she could do a good job, but what if she couldn't answer the interviewer's questions correctly? She really needed this job.

Sheila was beginning to talk herself out of the job. Maybe she was just trying to keep from getting her hopes up so that she wouldn't be disappointed when she didn't get the job.

"I wonder if I should tell someone I'm here," she thought. "I guess I'll just sit here and wait for someone to call me. At least I'm here on time. I wonder how many other people are applying for this job? Probably a lot. They probably all have experience, too. I wish the school would just find us a job like they did for the co-op part of our program. Where's my résumé? Good—here it is in my purse."

Sheila kept her eyes down. As she waited, she noticed that she had a stain on the cuff of her blouse. "Oh well, maybe no one will notice. I'll just have to keep my hand over the stain. I won't shake hands unless I have to. Hopefully, the interviewer won't notice the stain. It's not going to make any difference, anyway. They've probably already decided to give the job to someone else."

What kind of first impression do you think Sheila will make on the interviewer?

A   T A L K   W I T H   D R .   W A I T L E Y

Dr. Waitley focuses on self-projection: the ability to make dreams a reality by demonstrating your inner feelings of confidence and self-worth.

What Is Self-Projection?

Self-Projection is using your confidence and optimism to make good things happen. It is working toward the goal of feeling good about yourself; it is planning your successes. It is being optimistic in the face of all odds and thinking in a positive way, visualizing good things. Self-projection also involves **self-expectancy**. It is the idea that whatever you spend the most energy thinking about is what will come to pass, whether it is something you fear or something you desire. Self-expectancy takes the thoughts, feelings, and images of your subconscious and commits them to action.

Winners use self-projection to make good things happen.

Winners expect to win. They know that luck, chance, or good fortune may play a part, but only if they are ready and available to receive that good luck. Winners look at life as a game, not a gamble. They expect to win for three reasons:

1. *Desire.* They want to win.
2. *Self-control.* They can make it happen.
3. *Preparation.* They are ready to win.

Prepared for Success

If an individual is not prepared, he or she is not taking advantage of a situation. Opportunities are always around, but only those who are prepared can truly use them. Winners are better prepared than the rest.

Winners in sports expect to win their events. They know they are the best, and they focus all their energies on proving it. Doubters do not win, and Winners do not doubt. Swimmer Pablo Morales knew he would win a gold medal in the 1992 Summer Olympics, and that is just what he did.

Winners expect the best.

Everyone tends to receive what he or she expects in the long run. You may or may not get what you *deserve,* but you will nearly

always get what you expect. Winners expect to succeed, have financial security, enjoy good health, and have happy relationships.

Stress and Success

We know that our thoughts affect our bodies. Some studies have
shown that stressful life changes can come before an illness or accident. When we feel fear, our bodies can react by producing fewer
antibodies that fight illness. The body's immune system, which fights
infection and disease, may be affected by emotional changes. An
emotionally upset person is also more likely to have an accident.

Stress can lower a body's defenses and make it susceptible to illness.

> There are many examples of self-fulfilling prophecies, and some
can be quite dramatic. Dr. Herbert Benson told the story of a young
aborigine in Australia whose mind seemed to have direct control
over his body. During a journey, the man slept at an older friend's
home. For breakfast, the friend prepared a meal of wild hen, a food
the young were prohibited from eating by the elder tribesmen. The
young man asked if the meal was wild hen and the host said no. The
young man then ate the meal and left on his journey. Several years
later, when the two met again, the older friend asked the young man
whether he now would eat wild hen. The young man said he would
not since he had been ordered not to. The older friend laughed and
told him how he had been tricked into eating it years ago. The young
man became so upset that he was dead within 24 hours.

> Today support groups for cancer patients often provide not only
comfort but an environment that breeds a positive attitude toward
fighting the disease. Doctors often say that a patient's attitude can be
a big factor in his or her recovery. Some feel "thinking well can make
you well." There are thousands of former open-heart surgery patients
who are living proof that their outlook toward total recovery made
all the difference.

The Drug of Optimism

Feeling positive or optimistic is an important trait in a Winner. Dis-
coveries about the brain may explain what can help foster certain
positive feelings. The body makes morphinelike proteins called
endorphins. These proteins can reduce the feeling of pain and cause
a person to feel better. Studying them may help us understand why
we feel joy and depression.

Winners see problems as opportunities to challenge ability and determination. Winners use optimism (the ability to look for the positive in all situations) to fulfill their own futures. They seem to create good self-fulfilling prophecies to make the right things happen.

Winners see opportunities rather than problems.

Winners are self-made people because it is their own feelings of optimism and positive expectations that make them what they are. The enthusiasm of optimistic people is contagious; you can "catch" a healthy attitude by being around someone who is upbeat. Winners carry themselves in a way that makes them fun to be around. They like themselves and like others, too.

Projecting Self-Worth

Self-esteem comes through with a smile, which is the universal language that opens doors. A smile is the light in your window that tells others there is a caring and sharing person inside. Self-projection is the way we introduce ourselves to others. Winners always give their own names first, whether on the phone or in person. By stating your name up front, you are projecting self-worth and showing you are worth remembering.

Winners show that they feel good about themselves.

In person, you put out your hand to shake another's, showing that you are giving value to that person. This tradition began in ancient times as a double-hand clasp, showing that a weapon was not concealed. Anyone who would not shake hands was looked at with suspicion.

Also important is how we shake hands. Think about handshakes you have received from others. Which do you react positively to? A firm handshake (not a tight grip, not a limp hand) should be your goal to convey the impression of a confident person.

We need to realize that we project our feelings on the outside. When we do not feel well physically, we do not look well to others. So when we do not feel good about ourselves emotionally or mentally, we may not make a very good first impression.

Your Appearance

Studies have shown how important appearance is in life. When people are well groomed and dressed in clean clothes, they are treated better by their classmates and teachers. They feel attractive and therefore project a better image. Other studies have shown that some of the most beautiful people are less satisfied with themselves, less well adjusted, and less happy in later life.

Winners feel self-confident when they look their best.

Obviously, we cannot choose what looks we inherit from our parents. We can choose how we take care of our health and appearance and what we do to enhance them. Like it or not, we leave a lasting impression with our appearance. And we behave according to the way we think we look rather than the way we actually look. Those of us who take care of ourselves, and who learn to accept and be satisfied with ourselves, are the real self-fulfilled Winners in life.

Verbal Communication

The way you project or present yourself to others develops your image and can affect your self-projection. People are "senders," showing their thoughts and feelings to others. "Receivers" in our subconscious absorb this speechless communication. Winners take full responsibility for being certain that others understand what they are saying. They might give you examples, ask you what you think, or put what they said in different words.

Winners take responsibility for effective communication with others.

Winners keep things straightforward and simple. Winners speak in clear language, so listeners will understand their message. Winners ask questions to draw the other person out. When Winners pick up the telephone, they want to help the person on the other end; they have concern for others, not just for themselves. You know how uncomfortable you would feel if the person speaking to you on the phone was interested only in himself or herself and not in what you needed to know or say.

Nonverbal Communication

Nonverbal communication is "speaking" without words. It is body language, facial expressions, and hand movements. Winners listen to the total person. They observe body language, realizing that folded or crossed arms sometimes mean the listener is defensive. They understand that hands on hips may show aggressiveness. Winners watch the eyes, which can look down or away, showing a self-conscious attitude or guilt. They see eyes that can show surprise or anger. They listen to tone of voice, nervous laughter, or excited chatter.

No matter what the nonverbal cue may be, the most important nonverbal message will be your self-confidence. A head held high, good eye contact, good posture, and a firm handshake will all project your self-assurance.

Did you know that you can communicate nonverbally in a telephone conversation? A smile really does affect the tone of your voice and could be the difference between making a good or poor impression.

Body language communicates attitudes.

Winners accept that someone else's view may be different from their own and still be important. A Winner says, "I understand your idea. However, I would like to tell you why my position may be different from your own."

A Winning First Impression

Winners use the first four minutes of an encounter to make a good impression.

You can always spot a Winner when he or she walks into a room. Winners project a warm glow, a presence that can be like a magnet to others. Their healthy self-esteem comes through from the inside out. People respond to others with a gut-level feeling that is instantaneous. First impressions are powerful and lasting. Four minutes is all it takes to project a good or bad first impression. Many careers, top jobs, and sales deals are decided very early in the interview based on "gut feeling" and how the person projected himself or herself. How you project yourself when meeting someone for the first time is very important and involves direct eye contact, a smile, a handshake, and good listening skills.

The Values of a Winner

It seems popular to show off the things we buy and own to prove our worth. Actually, this need to show off expensive possessions only displays low self-esteem. Winners may not always be able to afford the most expensive things, but they always do the best with what they can afford. Their high self-esteem makes it unnecessary for them to prove their worth to others by showing off what they can buy. We do not have to depend on a house, car, or clothes to tell the world who we are. Does it really matter whose name is on the label if the clothes are clean and look nice?

Winners do not need to impress others with material possessions.

Winners make good use of their minds, skills, and talents. They project self-respect and respect for others and healthy self-esteem in their appearance. Project yourself every day as a Winner!

Let's take a closer look at some of the points Dr. Waitley discussed and learn how to use the principle of self-projection in our everyday lives.

The Importance of Self-Projection

Self-projection is having the self-confidence to achieve your goals and displaying that confidence in everything you do. It is expecting to do well, expecting to succeed, and projecting your successful self-image. It is letting others know you are going to succeed. What you believe will happen is likely to be what you make happen. With positive thinking, you can make positive things happen for yourself and those around you.

Projecting Good Health

Dr. Waitley writes that, sometimes, expecting to get sick might actually make you sick. Remember the story of the young Australian man? In this extreme case, the healthy young man had convinced himself so strongly that he was going to die that he did just that. This of course is a very unusual case, but we can witness the power of the mind in more common ways every day.

Your mind can make you sick or make you well.

A case in point is the use of placebos. **Placebos** are harmless sugar pills that the patient is told are real medicine. In many cases, patients will respond just as well to a placebo as they do to the actual medication. The patients believe the pills are real, and that belief is a very powerful thing.

People with asthma (an illness that makes it very hard to breathe) often find relief from their attacks simply by learning to relax deeply and think calming thoughts. Obviously, our thoughts can have a big influence on our health. The more we project good health, the better our chances are of feeling good.

Physical health is also affected by physical actions.

Remember, self-projection is a combination of positive thinking and positive action. Project positive, healthy thoughts and follow up with positive, healthy action. For you, this might mean breaking the smoking habit, cutting down on caffeine, or getting more exercise. How will you project good health today?

☞ *Projecting Success*

You will never reach your goals unless you work at them. Yet you might find that, hard as you work, your goals are still some distance away. In that case, the problem may be that you are not projecting success. Do others know that you are working toward your goals? As you move into the work world, you will find that this is very important.

Others will accept the image you project.

For instance, let's imagine that you are applying for a new job. You have worked hard in school and gotten good grades. You may just be the perfect person for the job of copy room clerk at the Cygnet Company. Your next task is to let the interviewer know you are the perfect person for the job. Remember, the company does not know much about you or what kind of person you are; and you have only four minutes to make that important first impression. Studies have shown that is how long it takes to make a first impression. The first impression is the lasting one.

Now imagine you do not feel well the morning of the interview. You are tired. You do not feel like dressing up; besides, you have heard that the company is very casual. You forgot to go to the library yesterday to research the company. What are your chances of getting the job?

The Cygnet Company is not going to take your word for it that you are the right person for the job. You have to show them. If you walk into the room tired and poorly dressed, the interviewer will soon be looking forward to the next applicant.

☞ *Making a Good Impression*

In her book *Career Directions*, Donna J. Yena lists four questions you should ask yourself when you want to make a good first impression:

- What do I look like?
- What do I sound like?
- What do I say?
- How well do I listen?

Making a good first impression is important not only for job interviews, but for many other occasions. Whenever you are meeting and talking with people, that first impression counts. Dr. Waitley talked about the different elements of a good impression: appearance, verbal communication, and nonverbal communication. The total of these elements should spell success to everyone you meet.

Appearance

It is extremely important that your outward appearance reflect your
winning attitude. Winners take pride in their appearance. They
would never dream of showing up to work or school in torn, dirty,
or sloppy clothes. Their hair is clean and combed, and if they wear
makeup, it is not overdone. Winners dress appropriately—that is,
they dress the right way for each occasion; they take their cues from
others. Winners know that dressing appropriately does not mean
giving up their own special qualities. It is perfectly possible to present yourself correctly *and* with a personal style all your own.

Verbal Communication

Communication is a very important skill in projecting success. How
well do you get your ideas across? Many people, when they are nervous, speak too quickly. Practice speaking slowly and clearly. No one
can tell what great ideas are in your brain unless you can learn to
express them clearly.

*Give some attention to
how you speak.*

Think about what you say. Are you getting your point across?
Are you repeating yourself or maybe not getting to the point at all? It
is important, in many jobs, to be able to present facts in a clear and
simple way. As a secretary, you might have to give directions to the
office over the phone. Suppose you are a data processor and sud-
denly your computer does not work. Would you be able to state
plainly to the repairperson what the problem is?

*Good listening involves
paying attention to what
the other person is saying.*

Communication is a two-way street. When one person is speaking, the other needs to be listening. Listening is not just hearing, it is
also paying attention. Some people simply "tune out" when they
should be listening. Unfortunately, because of this behavior, they
need the information repeated later. Winners are good listeners. They
keep their minds on what is being said. They know that good listening is an important skill to have as they work toward their goals.

Winners know that good communication is polite communication. They do not mumble, raise their voices, or interrupt when others
are speaking. They communicate in a way that is respectful of other
people's feelings. Making a good impression also means getting your
point across in a way that is pleasant for yourself and your listeners.
Is talking with you a pleasant experience?

*Speak as you would like
to be spoken to.*

Have you ever been in a large store, heard a cashier make an
announcement over the loudspeaker, and thought, "What did she
say?" Make sure others do not ask the same question when you are
finished speaking.

Nonverbal Communication

As Dr. Waitley told us, nonverbal communication is "speaking" without words. Nonverbal communication is one of the most important elements of making a good impression and projecting self-worth and success.

Show others your self-confidence through your body language.

How is your handshake? Winners shake hands firmly and with a smile. Have you ever been given a limp, tired handshake? What did you think about the person who gave it to you? Chances are that weak handshake did not help make a good impression on you. A firm handshake lets others know you are glad to meet them; it also says, I am confident.

Your posture also can project confidence. When your posture is good and you hold yourself straight and tall, you project self-worth and confidence. You look as though you are ready to meet a challenge. When you look ready to meet a challenge, people will feel confident in giving you challenges to face. Walk into a job interview straight and tall, knowing you are the best person for the job, and the interviewer will find it easier to see you that way, too. Remember, it is up to you to convince the interviewer that you are perfect for the job. If you do not project a winning attitude, there are many other candidates for the job who will.

Ask a friend, instructor, or family member to help you work on your nonverbal communication. Let people know you are a Winner without saying a word.

Make Your Own Luck

You may look at some Winners and say, "They are so lucky!" but luck usually has very little to do with it. Great jobs, good relationships, and happiness do not just fall into the laps of a lucky few. What seems to be luck is almost always just plain hard work. Winners make their own luck. They take an active role in creating their success. They let other people know they are ready for success.

In her novel *The Joy Luck Club,* author Amy Tan writes, "In America nobody says you have to keep the circumstances somebody else gives you." In other words, take those circumstances and exchange them for some you like better. The poet Emily Dickinson once said, "Luck is not chance, it's toil." She recognized that Winners work for their good luck.

Winners show others that they are willing to work for their good luck.

Entertainer Joan Rivers says that she has become her own version of an optimist. "If I can't get through one door, I'll go through another—or I'll make a door." Look around for a door and, if necessary, create one!

What Would a Winner Do?

Let's go back to the interview at the Cygnet Company. The morning of the interview, you are feeling tired and low. You have not really read much about the company, and you are thinking of just throwing on a pair of jeans and a sweater for the appointment because the company is very casual.

Remember, a good first impression may later be lowered, but rarely is a poor first impression raised.

Now ask yourself, what would a Winner do? First, you put on a clean pressed suit and style your hair, knowing that a casual dress code at a company is only for people who have already been hired. Remember, this company does not know anything about you, so that first impression is very important.

If you have not done any research on the company, you might leave early to stop at the library. A quick look at some business magazines and the help of a reference librarian should set you on the right track. You can write a few notes about the company and study them as you wait for your appointment.

Before you walk into the office, take several deep breaths of fresh air to wake yourself up. Walk into the interview thinking, win!

Get Ready for Success

Positive thinking does not promise success, but there is no success without it. "I believe very strongly in visualizing goals way beyond what seems humanly possible," says cartoonist Cathy Guisewite. "When my mother first suggested I submit some scribbles to a syndicate, I told her I knew nothing about comic strips. Mom said, 'So what? You'll learn.' When I pointed out that I didn't know how to draw, she said, 'So what? You'll learn.'" Without that positive thinking, encouragement, and confidence, Guisewite might never have turned those scribbles into the popular comic strip "Cathy."

It can be hard to expect success and project success when we stumble along the way. It is important to remember that working toward a goal means being persistent—that is, continuing to work toward that goal no matter what.

Winners are ready for success in all parts of their lives. They know that positive self-projection is not just for job interviews. Winners think positively about work, school, friends, family, and fun. They work hard to make good things happen, and they keep their eyes on their goals. Good luck seems to follow them wherever they go because they make it do so. They act like Winners even when they do not feel like Winners, and that is the key to their success.

S C E N E

8–2

◦

S H E I L A ' S   S T O R Y

Sheila projects confidence and finds success.

Sheila had set herself up for failure even before she walked into the interviewer's office. She was not hired, and Sheila went to speak with her placement adviser.

Sheila had made several mistakes before she even arrived at Rolling Hills Nursing Home. She had not taken the time to dress well for the interview so she would make a good impression. She hadn't researched the facility at the library. One of the most important items for a job interview—her résumé—was folded up in her purse. Worst of all, she had left her self-confidence at home.

Sheila had a long talk with her placement adviser about the importance of self-confidence. Sheila remembers one thing in particular that the adviser said: "Many times, just acting as though you have confidence will bring it back to you if you've lost it. Employers like to see confident people. No matter how low you might feel, it's important to project that confidence anyway. Act like a Winner, think like a Winner, be a Winner."

Sheila thought a lot about this advice when she got ready for her next interview. She planned what she'd wear the night before, and she dressed that morning in a nice business suit. In her briefcase, she had an updated résumé and some notes she'd written at the library about the facility and the good publicity it had received recently.

She did her best not to let negative thoughts and fears get in her way. She wore a confident smile and radiated an attitude that said, "I'm the best person for the job!" Armed with a positive attitude and all the right tools for a successful interview, Sheila got the job.

1. Do you agree with the concept of self-fulfilling prophecy? Can you cite any examples from your own experience?

2. Have you ever shown your yearbook to a friend and pointed out the people you consider to be the best looking? Has your friend agreed with you? Can you look at the pictures objectively to separate the appearance (your friend's only information) from the person's personality (that you are familiar with)? What does this tell you about Winners?

3. What steps can you take to make your own "luck"?

4. Do you feel attractive? Write about the reasons you do or don't. Do some clothes make you feel more attractive than others? What can you do to make yourself feel more attractive? What do your clothes say about you? Do they express your personality in a positive way? Why or why not? Think of ways your clothes can help you to project a winning attitude. What are some changes you need to make in your wardrobe for your new career when you graduate and find a job?

5. How can an actor or actress be appealing to you in one role and, with little help from makeup, be unappealing to you in another role?

Communication

_____

Instructions:

1. *Rate your communication skills. Next to each item listed below, indicate whether you use the skill (1) rarely, (2) sometimes, or (3) always.*

_____   When I'm speaking to someone face to face, I maintain eye contact.

_____   When I'm listening to someone else speak, I maintain eye contact.

_____   When I'm having a face-to-face conversation, my body language is friendly and relaxed.

_____   I'm careful not to interrupt when others are speaking.

_____   I take accurate phone messages when others are not home to receive their calls.

_____   When I answer the phone, I say hello and let callers know whom they're talking to.

_____   I know how to read others' body language, even when it differs with what they say.

_____   In class, I raise my hand before I answer a question.

_____   In school, I'm careful to keep my voice down when other students are studying nearby.

_____   I'm respectful when I speak to my instructors and the school staff.

_____   When a lot of people are talking at once, I don't raise my voice, but wait quietly until it's my turn to speak.

_____   When I'm introduced to someone new, I smile and give him or her a firm handshake.

_____   I stand straight when I enter a room.

_____   If I walk into a gathering in which I don't know anybody, I walk up to someone who appears friendly and introduce myself.

_____   People tell me I'm a good listener.

_____   I enjoy talking to other people.

_____   I can follow oral and written directions.

_____   I know how to argue without getting angry or abusive.

_____   It's easy for me to see someone else's point of view.

_____   I make a good first impression.

2. *What skills do you need to brush up on? From the list (Step 1), write the items rated 1 in the left-hand column below.*

_____   _____

_____

_____

_____   _____

_____

_____

_____   _____

_____

_____

_____   _____

_____

_____

3. *Work with another student in your class. Discuss ways that each of you can improve your communication skills (Step 2). Suggestions:*

    a. Start by comparing your lists.
    b. Write the word *hold* beside any item that appears on both lists.
    c. Talk about the unmarked items on first one list, then the other. Include in your discussion whether the other person sees you as you see yourself. Compare your self-image with the image others may have of you.
    d. Write ideas for improving communication on the lines at the right as you end discussion on each item.
    e. Finally, work on the items marked *hold* with your partner. You're learning to learn from your peers.

4. *Set up an appointment with your partner (Step 3) within the next week to talk about your progress in improving communication skills.*

Communication and Relationships

Instructions:

1. _In the spaces below, write some of the good things about your relationships with the people listed. Then write some ways each relationship could be improved. Finally, decide what communication skills you will work on to make that improvement._

    Example: My family
    What's good: My sister and I have fun shopping.
    What could be better: She yells at me if I come into the room when she's on the phone.
    Communication skills to work on: Knocking before I come into the room.

My partner

What's good: _____

What could be better: _____

Communication skills to work on: _____

_____

My family

What's good: _____

What could be better: _____

Communication skills to work on: _____

_____

My friends

What's good: _____

What could be better: _____

Communication skills to work on: _____

_____

My instructors

What's good: _____

What could be better: _____

Communication skills to work on: _____

_____

My co-workers

What's good: _____

What could be better: _____

Communication skills to work on: _____

_____

2. *Review the areas that need improvement (could be better) and communication skills (to work on) listed in Step 1. Do you see any similarity in the things you've listed? Explain.*

_____

_____

3. *Can the five problems and skills noted in Step 1 be combined? Instead of needing to work on five different communication skills, could you work on, say, three skills to solve all five problems? For example, you may notice that two problems (could be better) have to do with poor listening on your part. By improving your listening skills, you would be attacking both problems at once. How many different communication problems and skills did you note (in Step 1)? _____ List each different communication skill. (Some lines below may be left blank.)*

_____

_____

_____

_____

4. *For each skill listed (Step 3), write an action you must take to start working on that skill.*

_____

_____

_____

_____

5. *Copy these actions (Step 4) on your weekly to-do list (see Activity 7–5). You will set priorities on these to-do items along with other items on that list.*

Self-Improvement

You have already taken many, many steps toward self-improvement. Can you think of more little changes that could make a big difference in how you're viewed by other people? How others view you is important because it greatly affects how you feel about yourself.

Instructions:

1. *Strategies for self-improvement are listed below. Check each "I will" statement that applies to you.*

_____ I will say thank-you when I receive a compliment.

_____ I will smile more often.

_____ I will start leaving 10 minutes earlier for my appointments, so I know I'll be there on time.

_____ I will speak in a positive way to everyone I meet.

_____ I will dress in a way that lets people know how good I feel about myself.

2. *In the spaces below, list other things you will do to improve yourself—things that affect how others see you.*

I will_____

I will_____

I will_____

I will_____

I will_____

I will_____

3. *How will you remind yourself to do these things until they become habits? (**Hint:** Are you still using your positive self-talk statement (Activity 4–4) regularly and often? Remember to update the card every couple weeks. Always write into the new statement those things you want to improve.*

_____

_____

_____

_____

Dealing with Problems

Instructions:

1. _List two problems in your life right now. Then write why each one is difficult._

Problem A: _____

Why it's difficult: _____

Problem B: _____

Why it's difficult: _____

2. _Now pretend that these items were written by another student in the class. Write some possible solutions to the problems that you might suggest to that person._

Advice on Problem A: _____

_____

Advice on Problem B: _____

_____

3. _Do another person's problems seem smaller or easier to deal with than your own problems? Explain._

_____

_____

_____

4. _Is it easier to see problems as opportunities when they belong to someone else? Explain why or why not._

_____

_____

_____

5. _Write a one-sentence summary of what you learned as a result of this activity._

_____

_____

The Wheel of Life Comes Full Circle, Part 1

Instructions:

1. Read each of the 24 items on the following list.
2. Decide whether the statement is not true, somewhat true, or very true.
3. Circle a number 1 (not true) to 10 (very true) to show how true the statement is for you.

	Not True			Somewhat True				Very True		
1. I go to movies, restaurants, and so on, with friends.	1	2	3	4	5	6	7	8	9	10
2. I spend time thinking positively.	1	2	3	4	5	6	7	8	9	10
3. I exercise each day.	1	2	3	4	5	6	7	8	9	10
4. I enjoy time with my spouse or a special friend.	1	2	3	4	5	6	7	8	9	10
5. I have set goals for earning and spending money.	1	2	3	4	5	6	7	8	9	10
6. I am satisfied with my career choice and my career progress so far.	1	2	3	4	5	6	7	8	9	10
7. I am involved in community affairs.	1	2	3	4	5	6	7	8	9	10
8. I enjoy reading books or magazines.	1	2	3	4	5	6	7	8	9	10
9. I belong to a club or social group.	1	2	3	4	5	6	7	8	9	10
10. I have set personal goals—certain things that I want to do and to be.	1	2	3	4	5	6	7	8	9	10
11. I eat healthful foods.	1	2	3	4	5	6	7	8	9	10
12. I write or call family members from whom I am separated.	1	2	3	4	5	6	7	8	9	10
13. I earn the income I want.	1	2	3	4	5	6	7	8	9	10
14. I am involved in creative work—on the job or elsewhere.	1	2	3	4	5	6	7	8	9	10

	Not True	Somewhat True	Very True

15. I belong to a community association.

1 2 3 4 5 6 7 8 9 10

16. I attend workshops or special courses to increase my knowledge or skills.

1 2 3 4 5 6 7 8 9 10

17. I like to meet new people and to "hang out" or socialize.

1 2 3 4 5 6 7 8 9 10

18. I read books or take courses for the purpose of self-improvement.

1 2 3 4 5 6 7 8 9 10

19. I keep my weight under control; it's not more than 15 percent above the ideal weight for my gender, height, and age.

1 2 3 4 5 6 7 8 9 10

20. I have co-workers who are also friends.

1 2 3 4 5 6 7 8 9 10

21. I have a plan for saving money.

1 2 3 4 5 6 7 8 9 10

22. I have reached some, but not all, of my professional goals.

1 2 3 4 5 6 7 8 9 10

23. I volunteer from time to time for community projects.

1 2 3 4 5 6 7 8 9 10

24. I listen to audiocassette programs to learn more.

1 2 3 4 5 6 7 8 9 10

You will use the ratings that you have just completed later for an activity in Chapter 9. Reflect on the ratings you have marked to be sure they are accurate.

Nobody gets to live life backward. Look ahead—that's where your future lies.

☙

Ann Landers

Psychology of Success: Looking Back, Looking Ahead

⚭ *What Is Success?*

Success. What is it? Over the years, people have defined it as fortune, accomplishment, achievement, mastery, triumph, and victory. Such a small word with so many meanings!

In *Being the Best,* Dr. Waitley writes, "Success is not what you get, but what you continue to do with what you've got." He talks about success as being lifelong fulfillment. At the end of Chapter 7, you thought about the saying, "Happiness is the journey, not the destination." Everyone has different goals, and it is not the purpose of this book, or any book for that matter, to choose them for you. By now, though, you have a better idea of the personal qualities that are so important in achieving success. Added together, these winning qualities make up a person who knows what he or she wants and goes after it—in a way that is healthy, honest, and respectful of others.

All of these qualities have two things in common. First, they all involve positive thinking. Second, all of these qualities help to build self-confidence. Add those two together, and you spell success!

⚭ *The Principles of a Winner*

Let's go back for a moment to review the previous chapters and see how they all work together to help make you a Winner. If you don't remember or are unsure what some of the terms mean, check the glossary at the back of the book for definitions.

Chapter 2, Psychology of Self-Awareness

In Chapter 2, Dr. Waitley introduced us to **self-awareness**—knowing who we are and how we fit into the world around us. Self-awareness is the starting point on our success map.

Self-awareness helps us to figure out what kind of persons we are and what we want out of life. It helps us to understand our responsibilities—to ourselves, to others, and to our environment. It is the first building block to our goals. **Environmental self-awareness** helps us in **adapting** to events and people around us and in developing **empathy** toward others.

Self-awareness also lets us know what things might be a problem as we work toward our goals. **Physical self-awareness** helps us both to identify causes of **stress** and anger in our lives and to work to get rid of them. You learned several positive **escape responses** to deal with stress and anger.

We can each determine our potential through **mental self-awareness.** We don't have to be restricted by limitations that others place on us; we can each reach limits that only we know are possible.

What did you discover when you read Chapter 2? Maybe you discovered some things about yourself you did not know before. You might have thought of a dream you were never aware of before.

Chapter 3, Psychology of Self-Image

If self-awareness answers the question, "Where am I?" then **self-image** answers the question, "Who am I?" or, more exactly, "Who do I think I am?" When we studied the psychology of self-image in Chapter 3, we learned about the picture we have of ourselves in our mind's eye and how we can make that picture a positive one. The image we have of ourselves is the image we will project to others.

As we develop our positive self-images, we must often use our **conscious mind** to influence our **subconscious mind**. We must reject **self-defeating attitudes** and **labels** that limit our potential. We must be careful which **ideals** we choose because often they are not realistic in everyday life and to everyday people.

A positive self-image is the product of positive thinking and imagination. While reading Chapter 3, you may have begun to see yourself in a whole new light.

Chapter 4, Psychology of Self-Esteem

The next step on our success journey was a very important one. High self-esteem is the very heart of a winning attitude. **Self-esteem** is the value you place on yourself. You can aim for the highest goals in life only if you believe you are truly worthy of them. An important key to raising your self-esteem is your **self-acceptance**.

In Chapter 4, we learned many different ways to raise our self-esteem, including positive **self-talk**. We discovered that if we are able to practice **humility**, we can learn from our mistakes and move on without being called a failure. Remember that failure is an event, not a person. Maybe you were surprised to learn that so many people suffer from low self-esteem and that so many people have studied the problem. Were you surprised by how many ways you can raise your self-esteem?

Chapter 5, Psychology of Self-Discipline

When you know where you are and where you are going, the next step is learning how to get there. Chapter 5 showed us how. **Self-discipline** is the tool that keeps us on track. It is commitment to working toward a goal, one that you have chosen through your **self-determination**. These tools help us even in those moments in which we think we just do not care anymore.

We found that self-discipline has many of the elements we read about in Chapter 5: imagination, responsibility, and positive self-talk, among others. In Chapter 2, Dr. Waitley talked about dealing with stress. Here, he helped us learn how to break bad **habits** (including procrastination) and replace them with good ones. It is your **self-control** that gives you the **empowerment** over those bad habits. Don't let them control you. Self-discipline means putting things into action. While reading this chapter, did you become more aware of some habits you want to change?

Chapter 6, Psychology of Self-Motivation

Chapter 6 showed us how **self-motivation** can give us the jump-start we need to work even harder for success. We found out that many people are afraid of success, of failure, of taking risks. They fill their minds with negative self-talk. Self-motivation reminds us why we set our goals in the first place. It asks, What do you really want out of life? What do you **desire?** We learned about The Winner's Edge and more about positive self-talk. It is tough sometimes to keep on fighting, but **motivation** is what keeps us in the game. Were you surprised to read about the many troubles some famous Winners have gone through? Maybe you had thought everything just came easily to them.

Chapter 7, Psychology of Self-Direction

In Chapter 7, Dr. Waitley talked about **self-direction**. Self-direction keeps us on the right course by identifying our **purpose** and by showing us how to set **goals**. Successful goals are clear and realistic; long-term goals are made up of many short-term ones. We read about time and money management and about having a positive attitude.

If **happiness** is a journey, not a destination, then self-direction makes sure that our journey is traveled on the right path. What new goals did you set while you read this chapter?

Chapter 8, Psychology of Self-Projection

None of us achieve success entirely on our own. We always have to talk, work, and live with other people. Chapter 8, on **self-projection,** taught us how to project confidence in everything we do. It is important that others know about our winning attitude. Perhaps you did not know when you started the chapter about all the different ways we reveal ourselves to others without even saying a word. Communication is the tool by which we tell people, "I'm a Winner!"

If we set a high and achievable **self-expectancy**, our goals can become **self-fulfilling prophecies**.

Did you have any idea how important first impressions are? After reading this chapter, maybe you have decided to change the way you present yourself. Maybe you are walking a little taller, holding your head a little higher. You know now that the surest way to feel confidence is to project confidence. When you cannot think yourself into acting, act yourself into thinking.

We know that success can be measured only by what we want for ourselves; it cannot be determined by family, friends, or society. Likewise, we determine our attitudes. If we are to reach our goals, it is important that we not let anyone or anything damage the positive attitude we have chosen for ourselves.

Join the Winners' Circle

It also is very important that we build a support system around ourselves: a group of trusted relatives, friends, instructors, or advisers who will guide us and help us on our journeys. As you move in the direction of your goals, you will find that you become a part of other people's support systems. Your victories, defeats, and other experiences will help you guide those who are just beginning their journeys.

Dr. Waitley once called success "the progressive realization of goals that are worthy of the individual." What does this mean? First, it means that you value yourself highly and choose only goals that are deserving of your time and effort—goals that, when met, will make you a better person. Second, "progressive" means one goal follows another. Success is achieving many goals over a period of time; success is not tied to only one goal. Of course, "realization" means the achievement of dreams and goals.

Again we learn that happiness is in our journey. Happiness and success are not just about meeting goals but about enjoying yourself, liking yourself, and accepting yourself along the way. Winners do not have to be world-class athletes, famous actors, or millionaires. Winners are everyday people just like you, who want a better, happier life and are willing to work for it. They are enjoying life while they live it. It is now your turn to start the journey. With the lessons you have learned from this book and your own winning attitude, you are bound to succeed.

How do you measure success?

To laugh often and much;

To win the respect of intelligent people and the affection
    of children;

To appreciate beauty;

To find the best in others;

To leave the world a little better, whether by a healthy child,
    a garden patch, a redeemed social condition, or a job well
    done;

To know even one other life has breathed easier because you
    have lived—

This is to have succeeded.

Ralph Waldo Emerson

THOUGHT-PROVOKING QUESTIONS

1. How would you define success and happiness? How is it possible to make your own success and happiness? What steps can you take? Are you doing anything differently since reading this book?

2. Which principle of a winner meant the most to you? Write about how and why it did. Which one will take the most effort for you to achieve?

3. It has been said that "there are two great times of happiness—when you are haunted by a dream and when you realize it." Do you think sometimes it is as much fun working at goals as it is achieving them? Why or why not?

4. Have your goals changed since you began this book? Have you created some inner goals that only you can measure, as well as some outward goals that others will use to measure your success? Which are more important to you?

5. Now that you have learned how to create a winning attitude for yourself, how can you help others do the same thing? Remember Dr. Waitley's "double win" attitude (Chapter 2). What are you doing to help others be Winners, too?

The Wheel of Life Comes Full Circle, Part 2

Instructions:

1. You will need the ratings that you completed in Activity 8–5. For each of the 24 items, write the rating you gave it (1–10) on the correct line below.

Attitude

Item 2 _____

Item 10 _____

Item 18 _____

Total _____

Money

Item 5 _____

Item 13 _____

Item 21 _____

Total _____

Community

Item 7 _____

Item 15 _____

Item 23 _____

Total _____

Recreation

Item 1 _____

Item 9 _____

Item 17 _____

Total _____

Health

Item 3 _____

Item 11 _____

Item 19 _____

Total _____

Relationships

Item 4 _____

Item 12 _____

Item 20 _____

Total _____

Job/Career

Item 6 _____

Item 14 _____

Item 22 _____

Total _____

School

Item 8 _____

Item 16 _____

Item 24 _____

Total _____

2. *Record the total for each area in Step 1 on the wheel below. Using the numbers on the spokes of the wheel as a guide, shade the section of the wheel to match each total.*

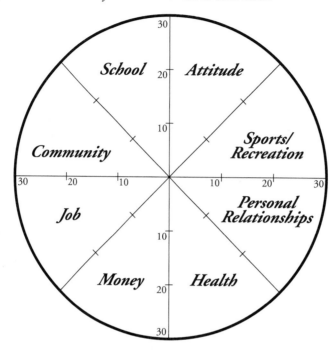

3. *Compare this wheel with the one(s) completed earlier (the Wheel of Life first appeared in Activity 2–3. In the meantime, you may have completed the activity again). Write a general description of (a) the ways you've changed and (b) how you expect to use what you've learned in your future.*

_____

_____

_____

_____

_____

_____

_____

_____

_____

_____

_____

S C E N E

9–1

J A C K ' S   S T O R Y

Portrait of a Winner

Jack is living his success story. He set his goals, followed his dream, and worked hard to graduate from school with a degree in hotel management. Along the way, some people told him he was aiming too high. Be content with what you have, they said. Jack knew that he wanted more out of life. He wanted a career that made the most of his talents. He wanted to feel he was doing important work. He wanted to be the very best he could be.

So Jack ignored the negative thoughts of others. Instead, he focused on his own positive thoughts. He asked for the support of family and friends when he needed it, too. He visualized his goal and did not let anything keep him from it. The day Jack got his diploma was one of the happiest in his life. Now Jack is doing what he really loves. He likes making a stay in his hotel a pleasurable experience for travelers.

It was hard work for Jack to get where he is. He had a schedule full of classes, homework, and part-time jobs. Fortunately, he quickly learned the importance of self-discipline, self-motivation, and a winning attitude. These are some of the qualities that make him such a success in his career today.

Jack has a positive attitude about the future, too. He knows that he can apply his determination and confidence to any goal he sets. Jack expects success and works for it. Some day he plans to own his own hotel. He is a Winner!

Select Bibliography

Baltus, Rita. *Personal Psychology for Life and Work.* New York: McGraw-Hill, 1988.

Branden, Nathaniel. *The Power of Self-Esteem.* Deerfield Beach, FL: Heath Communications, 1992.

———. *The Six Pillars of Self-Esteem.* New York: Bantam Books, 1994.

Brownmiller, Susan. *Femininity.* New York: Linden Press/Simon & Schuster, 1984.

Burns, David D. *Feeling Good: The New Mood Therapy.* New York: William Morrow, 1980.

Covey, Stephen R. *First Things First.* New York: Simon & Schuster, 1994.

Dyer, Wayne. *Your Erroneous Zones.* New York: Funk & Wagnall's, 1976.

Frankl, Victor. *Man's Search for Meaning.* 3rd ed. New York: Simon & Schuster, 1984.

Gellman, Meryle, and Diane Gage. *The Confidence Quotient.* New York: World Almanac Publications, 1985.

Gillespie, Peggy Roggenbuck, and Lynn Bechtel. *Less Stress in 30 Days.* New York: Plume Books/New American Library, 1986.

Givens, Charles J. *Super Self: Doubling Your Personal Effectiveness.* New York: Simon & Schuster, 1993.

Helmstetter, Shad. *What to Say When You Talk to Your Self.* Scottsdale, AZ: Grindle Press, 1986.

Lewis, Robert T. *Taking Chances: The Psychology of Losing.* Boston: Houghton Mifflin, 1979.

Peale, Norman Vincent. *Why Some Positive Thinkers Get Powerful Results.* New York: Ballantine Books, 1986.

Sher, Barbara, with Barbara Smith. *I Could Do Anything: If Only I Knew What It Was.* New York: Delacorte Press, 1994.

Siegel, Bernie. *Peace, Love & Healing.* New York: HarperCollins, 1989.

Timm, Paul R. *Successful Self-Management: A Psychologically Sound Approach to Personal Effectiveness.* Los Altos, CA: Crisp Publications, 1987.

Von Oech, Roger. *A Whack on the Side of the Head.* Rev. ed. New York: Warner Books, 1992.

Waitley, Denis. *The Psychology of Winning*. Chicago: Nightingale–Conant, 1978.

———.*The Winner's Edge*. New York: The New York Times, 1980.

———. *The Seeds of Greatness*. Old Tappan, NJ: Fleming H. Revell, 1982.

———. *The Double Win*. Old Tappan, NJ: Fleming H. Revell, 1984.

———. *Quantum Fitness: The Olympic Fitness Book*. New York: Simon & Schuster, 1984.

———. *The Joy of Working*. New York: Dodd, Mead, 1985.

———. *Winning the Innovation Game*. Old Tappan, NJ: Fleming H. Revell, 1986.

———. *Being the Best*. Nashville, TN: Thomas Nelson, 1987.

———. *Timing Is Everything*. Nashville, TN: Thomas Nelson, 1992.

———. *The New Dynamics of Winning*. New York: William Morrow, 1993.

Wells, Joel. *Who Do You Think You Are? How to Build Self-Esteem*. Chicago: The Thomas More Press, 1989.

Yena, Donna J. *Career Directions*. 3rd ed. Homewood, IL: Richard D. Irwin, 1997.

Ziglar, Zig. *Over the Top*. Nashville, TN: Thomas Nelson, 1994.

———. *See You at the Top*. New York: Pelican, 1984.

Glossary

adapting being flexible and open to the actions of others. (Chap. 2)

conscious mind the part of our minds that we use to make decisions based on information. (Chap. 3)

desire the need inside each person to want the reward. (Chap. 6)

empathy the awareness of, and sensitivity to, the feelings, thoughts, and experiences of others. (Chap. 2)

empowerment taking responsibility for your life; knowing you are in control and have the power to change things. (Chap. 5)

environmental self-awareness realizing that each human being on earth is a person with the equal right to fulfill his or her own potential in life. It is realizing that skin color, religion, birthplace, financial status, or intelligence do not determine a person's worth or value. (Chap. 2)

escape response an action or behavior that helps get your mind off your troubles. (Chap. 2)

goal the outcome you want. (Chap. 7)

habit a behavior that develops by being repeated over and over. (Chap. 5)

happiness a state of well-being and contentment that comes from living a worthwhile life. (Chap. 7)

humility the ability to accept correction and learn from errors. (Chap. 4)

labels statements we use to define who we are. (Chap. 3)

mental self-awareness knowing the potential within our own minds that is just waiting to be challenged. (Chap. 2)

motivation the force within us that drives us to do something. (Chap. 6)

physical self-awareness understanding that our bodies are machines whose performance depends on good health. (Chap. 2)

placebo harmless sugar pills that the patient is told are real medicine. (Chap. 8)

purpose what enables each of us to face up to difficult times and tragedies in our lives. (Chap. 7)

self-acceptance accepting responsibility for what happens in your life. (Chap. 4)

self-awareness the ability to look at yourself as you relate to your environmental, physical, and mental worlds. (Chap. 2)

self-control taking responsibility for your present and future actions. (Chap. 5)

self-defeating attitude anticipating failure before trying. (Chap. 3)

self-determination taking responsibility for determining the path your life travels. (Chap. 5)

self-direction setting a well-defined goal and working toward it. (Chap. 7)

self-discipline teaching yourself to do the things that are necessary to reach your goals without becoming sidetracked by bad habits. (Chap. 5)

self-esteem confidence and satisfaction in yourself. (Chap. 4)

self-expectancy the idea that whatever you spend the most energy thinking about is what will come to pass. (Chap. 8)

self-image the way we see ourselves in our minds. (Chap. 3)

self-projection using your confidence and optimism to make good things happen. (Chap. 8)

self-talk telling your subconscious mind that you are doing fine. (Chap. 4)

stress any physical, emotional, or chemical factor that causes tension. (Chap. 2)

subconscious mind the part of our mind that stores the emotions and sensations we are not quite aware of, the feelings that are just under the surface. (Chap. 3)

visualization the ability to see success, feel success, and experience success before actually completing the activity. (Chap. 3)

*I*ndex

Abbott, Jim, 111

Activities
    for change, 97-100
    communications, 231-234
    enhancing self-awareness, 29-43
    improving self-esteem, 89-105
    positive speech, 101-102, 159-162
    procrastination, 197-198
    self-direction, 197-210
    self-image, 61-71
    self-motivation, 159-176
    for self-projection, 231-240
    stress reduction, 37-39, 41-43
    for success, 251-252
    time management, 123-125
    understanding self-discipline,
      123-139

Adapting, 244
    to change, 18-19
    self-awareness and, 14

Admire a Hero (activity), 65

Admire Me (activity), 71

Adrenaline, 22

Alcoholism, 20, 80

Anger, 15, 22-23

Appearance, 218-219

Attendance Chart (activity), 135-136

Attitudes
    effects on success, 217
    happiness and, 191-192
    positive, 117-118, 225
    self-defeating, 49, 245
    self-image and, 51-52
    winning, 221-226

Balanced Living (activity), 33-34

Baltus, Rita, 149

Behavior, 114

Being the Best (Waitley), 244

Benson, Dr. Herbert, 217

Bibliography, 257-258

Body language, 219-220, 224

Bogomoletz, Alexander, 140

Braille, Louis, 111

Budgets, 190-191

Career Directions (Yena), 150, 222

Carey, Jim, 84

Challenges, 14-15, 82

Change, 18-19, 97-100

Choices, 114-115

Clothing, 55, 222, 223, 225

Comfort zone, 152

Communication (activity), 231-232

Communication and Relationships
(activity), 233-234

Communications; *see also* Body
language
    activities for, 231-232, 233-234
    listening as part of, 223
    projecting winning images with,
      219, 223
    about self-worth, 218-220

Compliments, 78-79

Confidence, 77, 225-226, 244

Conscious mind, 51, 245

Controlling your life, 114-119

Cortisol, 22

Covey, Stephen R., 56-57

Creativity, 55-57

Daydreaming, 115-116

Dealing with Problems (activity), 237

Desire, 110, 246
    concentrating on, 145
    motivation and, 144

Devers, Gail, 147

Dickinson, Emily, 224

Discipline; *see* Self-discipline

Do You Resist Change? (activity), 97-100

Dravecky, Dave, 147

Draw a Tree (activity), 199

Dream Job (activity), 67-70

Drug abuse, 20

Egocentric outlooks, 83

Einstein, Albert, 50

Ellerbee, Linda, 24

Emerson, Ralph Waldo, 2, 248

Empathy, 13, 18

Empowerment, 117, 246

Endorphins, 217-218

Environmental self-awareness, 12-13,
17-18, 244

Escape responses, 20, 81, 245

Ewing, Sam, 72

Exaggerating problems, 83

Exercise, 15, 20-21

Failure
    building self-esteem and, 84-85
    fear of, 145, 153
    taking risks and, 145-146

Fear
    of failure, 145, 153
    overcoming, 146
    of success, 49, 145

Feelings
    empathy and, 13, 18
    endorphins and, 217-218
    visualizations and, 152

Flexibility, 18-19

Frankl, Viktor, 183-184

Fromm, Eric, 148

Glossary, 259

Goals
    achieving, 81-82, 116-117, 145, 183,
      246
    comfort zone, 152
    determining your, 182, 184-188
    examining, 150-151

Goals—*Cont.*
  happiness and, 191-192
  overcoming procrastination, 153
  progressive realization of, 247
  self-projection and, 221
  support systems to reach, 118, 247
  time management and, 188-189
  visualizing, 151-152
Grisham, John, 24
Guisewite, Cathy, 225

Habits, 56-57, 246
  breaking bad, 116-117
  defined, 110
  self-control and, 113
Handshakes, 218
Happiness, 185, 191-192, 246
Health, 22, 84
Holmes, Oliver Wendell, Sr., 8
Human suffering, 183-184
Humility, 77, 245

Ideals, about self, 54-55
Identity, 54
Imagination, 50
Imagine That. . . (activity), 61-62
Impressions, 218-220, 222-225, 247
Increasing Self-Awareness (activity),
  29-31
Irving, Washington, 178
It's About Time! (activity), 207-210

James, William, 191
Jordan, Michael, 52
Joy Luck Club, The (Tan), 224
Joyner-Kersee, Jackie, 52

Kabat-Zinn, Jon, 54
Keller, Helen, 111
Kitchman, A. L., 44

Labels, self-image and, 49-50, 54, 245
Landers, Ann, 242
Laughter, 21
Learning, 48
L'Engle, Madeleine, 56-57

Lincoln, Abraham, 154
Listening, 115, 223
Look Who's Making Headlines (activity),
  205-206
Luck, 224-225
Lunden, Joan, 83

Man's Search for Meaning (Frankel),
  183-184
Marginal notes, 6
Maslow, Abraham, 148-149
Material possessions, making impres-
  sions and, 220
McMahon, Tim, 146
Memory, 48
Mental self-awareness, 16, 23-24, 245
Michener, James, 114
Mind; *see also* Thoughts
  conscious and subconscious, 245
  self-image and, 51
Mistakes, 77-78
Money management, 190-191
Morales, Pablo, 216
Motivation; *see* Self-motivation
Music, 21

Napoleon, 50
Negative escape responses, 20, 81
Negative thoughts, 82-83
Nightingale, Earl, 14
Nonverbal communications, 219-220,
  224

O'Connor, Sandra Day, 155
Opening quotes, 5
Optimism, winners and, 217-218
Overcoming Obstacles (activity), 131-133
Overeating, 20
Over the Top (Ziglar), 101

Peale, Norman Vincent, 187
Pen Pal, The (activity), 63-64
Personal Motivation (activity), 167-168
Personal Stressors and Relievers
  (activity), 41-43
Physical self-awareness, 14-15, 19-23,
  244

Placebos, 221
Positive actions; *see also* Activities
  for avoiding stress, 23
  building self-esteem, 84-85
  self-projection and, 175-176, 221
Positive emotions, 217-218
Positive Projection (activity), 175-176
Positive Self-Talk (activity), 101-102,
  159-162
Positive self-talk; *see* Self-talk
Positive tension, 145
Positive thinking, 187, 225-226
Powell, Gen. Colin, 117
Problems, overcoming, 187-188
Procrastination, 153, 197-198
Punctuality, 190
Punishment, 148-149
Purpose, in life, 183-184, 246

Reactivity, 23
Reality checks, 21
Relaxation, 21
Responsibility
  self-discipline and, 117
  self-esteem and, 83
  for your life, 112
Rewards, 148-149
Rice, Jerry, 153
Risk, as opportunity, 145-146
Rivers, Joan, 225
Role models, 155
Ruth, Babe, 154

Sabotaging success, 49
Scenes, 6
  self-awareness, 10-11, 26-27
  self-direction, 180-181
  self-discipline, 108-109, 120-121
  self-esteem, 74-75, 86-87
  self-image, 46-47, 58-59
  self-motivation, 142-143, 156-157
  self-projection, 214-215, 228-229
  of success, 254-255
Schwarzkopf, Gen. H. Norman, 106
Seeds of Greatness (Waitley), 23-24
Self-acceptance, 78, 245
Self-awareness, 4, 9-43, 244
  activities for, 29-43
  adapting and, 14
  defined, 12
  Dr. Waitley on, 12-16
  empathy and, 13, 18

Self-awareness—*Cont.*
  environmental, 12-13, 17-18
  importance of, 17
  mental, 16, 23-24
  physical, 14-15, 19-23
  questions about, 28
  scenes about, 10-11, 26-27
  study objectives for, 9
  winning with, 17-25
Self-control, 111-119, 246
Self-defeating attitudes, 49, 245
Self-determination, 112, 246
Self-direction, 4, 179-210, 246
  achieving goals, 183, 186
  activities about, 197-210
  attitude and, 192
  defined, 182
  determining your goals, 182,
    184-185
  Dr. Waitley on, 182-185
  happiness, 185, 191-192
  long- and short-term goals, 186-188
  money management, 190-191
  overcoming problems, 187-188
  questions about, 196
  scenes about, 180-181, 194-195
  study objectives for, 179
  time management, 188-190
Self-discipline, 4, 107-139, 246
  activities about, 123-139
  breaking bad habits, 116-117
  choosing positive attitudes, 118
  controlling your life and, 111-113
  Dr. Waitley on, 110-113
  importance of, 114
  making choices, 114-115
  questions about, 122
  scenes about, 108-109, 120-121
  study objectives for, 107
  support systems for, 118
  time and, 115-116
  and visualization, 111
  winning with, 114-118
Self-esteem, 4, 73-105, 245
  activities about, 89-105
  building, 82-85
  creating support systems for, 85,
    247
  defined, 76
  Dr. Waitley on, 76-79
  high, 81
  importance of, 80
  learning to like yourself, 76-77
  low, 80-81
  questions about, 88
  reaching goals and, 145
  scenes about, 74-75, 86-87
  self-worth and, 77, 85
  studying, 80
  study objectives for, 73
  winning with, 80-86
Self-expectancy, 216, 247
Self-fulfilling prophecies, 217, 247

Self-image, 4, 45-71, 245
  activities for, 61-71
  Dr. Waitley on, 48-52
  ideals and, 54-55
  labels, 49-50, 54, 245
  learning and, 48
  questions about, 60
  reaching goals and, 145
  scenes about, 46-47, 58-59
  searching for identity, 54
  self-defeating attitudes and, 49
  study objectives for, 45
  subconscious mind and, 51
  using creativity to develop, 55-57
  visualization and, 56-57
  of winners, 50-57
Self-Improvement (activity), 235
Self-motivation, 4, 141-176, 246; *see also*
Self-talk
  activities about, 159-176
  comfort zone and, 152
  concentrating on successes, 154
  defined, 148
  desire and, 144
  Dr. Waitley on, 144-147
  overcoming procrastination, 153
  positive tension, 145
  questions about, 158
  role models and, 155
  scenes about, 142-143, 156-157
  self-talk and, 151
  setting goals, 150-151
  study objectives for, 141
  taking risks and, 145-146
  values, 149
  views on, 148-149
  and visualization, 151-152
  winning and, 146, 148-155
Self-projection, 4, 213-240, 247
  activities about, 231-240
  confidence, 225-226
  defined, 216
  Dr. Waitley on, 216-220
  good health, 221
  making good impressions, 218-220,
    222-225, 247
  making your own luck, 224-225
  material possessions and, 220
  positive attitudes, 217-218
  preparing for success, 216-217,
    225-226
  projecting success, 222
  questions about, 230
  scenes about, 214-215, 228-229
  stress and, 217
  study objectives for, 213
  winning attitudes and, 221-226
Self-talk, 245
  achieving goals with, 151
  activities for, 101-102, 159-162
  breaking bad habits, 116-117
  overcoming problems, 187-188
  practicing positive, 78-79, 101-102,
    111-112

Self-worth
  communicating, 218-220
  self-esteem and, 77
  signs of, 85
Selye, Dr. Hans, 15
*Seven Habits of Highly Effective People,
The* (Covey), 56-57
Shriver, Maria, 24
Skinner, B. F., 148
SMART Goals (activity), 201-203
Standing Your Ground (activity), 163-165
Stress, 14-15, 244-245
  activities about, 37-39, 41-43
  dealing with, 19-21
  illness and, 217
  physical effects of, 22
  positive tension and, 145
  reducing, 20-21
Stress Test (activity), 37-39
Study objectives, 5
  for self-awareness, 9
  for self-direction, 179
  for self-discipline, 107
  for self-esteem, 73
  for self-image, 45
  for self-motivation, 141
  for self-projection, 213
Subconscious mind, 245
  self-image and, 51
Success, 244
  activities for, 251-252
  fear of, 49, 145
  how attitudes affect, 77-78, 154, 217,
    244
  motivation for, 147
  preparing for, 7, 154, 216-217, 225-
    226
  projecting, 222
  questions about, 249
  scenes of, 254-255
Success at Work (activity), 169-173
Successful Self-Management, 149
Support systems
  for achieving goals, 118, 247
  building self-esteem and, 85
  for solving problems, 187-188

Tan, Amy, 224
Tasks, dividing, 189-190
Test Your Self—Esteem (activity), 89-93
Thomas, Isaiah, 76-77
Thought-provoking questions, 6, 28,
60, 88, 122, 158, 196, 230
Thoughts
  concentrating on desires, 145
  negative, 82-83
  positive thinking, 221, 225-226
  slowing down, 21

Time-Demand Survey (activity), 123-125

Time management, 188-190
    activities for, 123-125
    disciplining, 115-116

Timm, Paul R., 149

To-Do Chart (activity), 137-139

Travis, Randy, 114

Twain, Mark, 116

Using Self-Discipline (activity), 127-129

Using this book, 4-7

U-Turns Allowed (activity), 103-105

Values, motivation and, 149

Valuing others, high self-esteem and, 81-82

Victim strategies, 113, 117

Visualization
    achieving goals with, 151-152
    changing self-imagery and, 56-57
    for self-discipline, 111

Von-Oech, Robert, 56

Waitley, Dr. Denis, 6, 23-24, 244, 247
    on self-awareness, 12-16
    on self-discipline, 110-113
    on self-esteem, 76-79
    on self-image, 48-52
    on self-motivation, 144-147
    on self-projection, 216-220

Watts, Alan, 18

Wells, Joel, 53, 84

Whack on the Side of the Head, A (von-Oech), 56

Wheel of Life (activities), 35-36, 239-240, 251-252

Who Do You Think You Are? (Wells), 53, 84

Why Some Positive Thinkers Get Powerful Results (Peale), 187

Williams, Dr. Redford, 22

Winfrey, Oprah, 147

Winners
    accepting compliments, 78-79
    body language and, 219-220, 224
    change and, 110
    characteristics of, 12-16
    communications by, 219, 223
    creating your own luck, 224-225
    desire and, 144
    goals for, 183-185

Winners—*Cont.*
    learning to like yourself, 76-77
    making a good impression, 218-220, 222-225, 247
    positive attitude of, 217-218
    positive self-talk, 78-79, 101-102, 111-112, 151, 187-188
    principles of, 244-247
    punctuality and, 190
    self-acceptance and, 78, 245
    self-awareness and, 17-25
    self-control and, 111-113
    self-discipline and, 114-118
    self-image and, 50-57
    self-motivation, 146, 148-155
    taking risks, 145-146

Winner's Edge, 146, 246

Winning, and self-expectancy, 216

Yena, Donna J., 150, 222

Your Values (activity), 95-96

Ziglar, Zig, 101